Textile Designs

Ideas and Applications

Textile Designs

Ideas and Applications

Joel Sokolov

Library of Applied Design

An Imprint of

PBC INTERNATIONAL, INC. ✦ NEW YORK

Distributor to the book trade in the United States and Canada:

Rizzoli International Publications Inc.
300 Park Avenue South
New York, NY 10010

Distributor to the art trade in the United States and Canada:

PBC International, Inc.
One School Street
Glen Cove, NY 11542
1-800-527-2826
Fax 516-676-2738

Distributed throughout the rest of the world:

Hearst Books International
1350 Avenue of the Americas
New York, NY 10019

Library of Congress Cataloging-in-Publication Data

Sokolov, Joel
    Textile designs: ideas and applications/by Joel Sokolov.
            p.   cm.
    Includes index.
    I. Textile design—United States—History—20th
century—Themes. motives. 2. Textile printing—United
States. I. Title.
    NK9500. S65 1991   91-26522
    677--dc20   CIP
    ISBN 0-86636-141-3

CAVEAT—Information in this text is believed accurate, and
will pose no problem for the student or the casual reader.
However, the author was often constrained by information
contained in signed release forms, information that could
have been in error or not included at all. Any misinformation
(or lack of information) is the result of failure in these
attestations. The author has done whatever is possible to
insure accuracy.

Color separation, printing and binding by
Toppan Printing Co. (H.K.) Ltd. Hong Kong

Typography by
TypeLink

10 9 8 7 6 5 4 3 2 1

Acknowledgments

Thanks to all the artists/designers who participated. Thanks to everyone at PBC International. Many thanks to Kevin Clark, John Wuchte, and my family and friends.

Contents

Introduction

Welcome to *Textile Designs: Ideas and Applications*. Prepare yourself to be pleasantly surprised by the exciting variety of designs for textiles and the ways they are utilized that you are about to explore.

From the unexpected, hand-painted, printed and appliqued textile to the excellent, commercial contract upholstery fabrics displayed in the following pages, you'll be impressed with the numerous interpretations of textile designs and their applications. One-of-a-kind quilts, site-specific installations, unique furnishings which include textiles, garments made with original textile designs, and preliminary drawings and paintings for textile designs are all included.

In preparing to assemble this book, I became more and more aware of the role textiles play in our lives: textiles touch our lives, literally, most of the time. We use textiles for utilitarian purposes but also to identify ourselves. Whether it's by a team logo or political statement displayed on our T-shirts, a polyester leisure suit, a uniform, a flag, the decor in our homes, or a work of art, we define ourselves, whether consciously or not, through textiles.

Textiles lend themselves to the expression of ideas. When we wear a certain fabric, when we observe the way light comes through a translucent set of curtains on a sunny day, or when we appreciate an art object created on or with textiles, we are affected by the experience.

Each of the works represented in this book is a fine example of inspired textile design and/or design with textiles. I'm sure you will be as impressed as I am with the artistry, skill and variety of work created by the talented artists and designers represented in the following pages.

Home and Personal Furnishings

Adam James
A Subsidiary of J.M. Lynne Company
Rifton, New York

DESIGNER
Adam James
DESIGN FIRM
Adam James Textiles
REPRESENTED BY
William Kent Schoenfisch

Adam James designs contract upholstery textiles specifically developed for high-wear, long-life contract applications. It is a subsidiary of J.M. Lynne Company.

TEXTILE
"Eternity-Cordura Group"
DESIGNER
Adam James
DESIGN FIRM
Adam James Textiles
USAGE
Contract Upholstery

"Eternity" is designed as an upholstery fabric made with DuPont Cordura high-performance nylon. It is available in a range of colors, textures, and patterns.

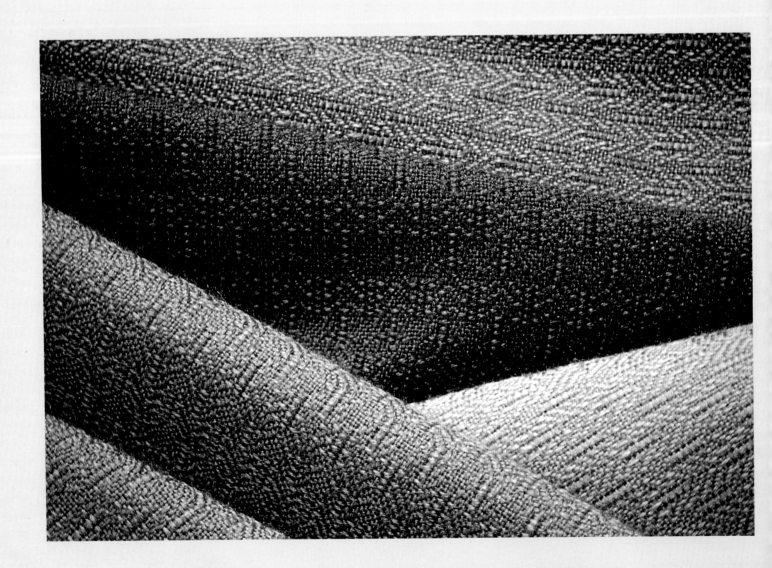

TEXTILE
"Sonata"
DESIGNER
Laura Deubler Mercurio
DESIGN FIRM
Adam James Textiles
USAGE
Contract Upholstery

"Sonata" is a complex twill design, whose warp and weft and pure color diagonal accents create a sense of movement reminiscent of wind-driven rain. A total of 24 colorways are available. This handsome textile is spun of 100 percent worsted long staple nylon.

TEXTILE
"Mirage-Cordura Group"
DESIGNER
Adam James
DESIGN FIRM
Adam James Textiles
USAGE
Contract Upholstery

"Mirage," another textile design from
the "Cordura Group," is suited for
healthcare, hospitality, and general
office/public space seating applications. The Cordura nylon it is composed of exhibits abrasion resistance
equivalent to one million double rubs
on the Wyzenbeek test.

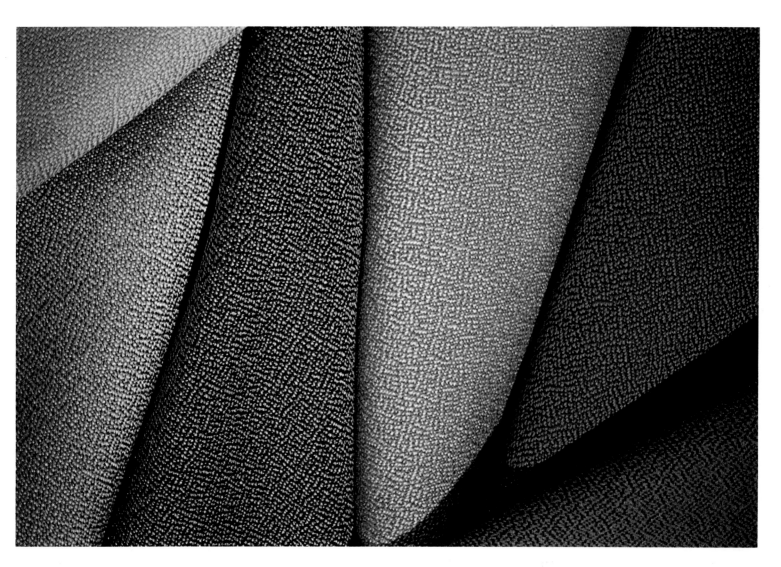

TEXTILE
"Ovation-Cordura Group"
DESIGNER
Adam James
DESIGN FIRM
Adam James Textiles
USAGE
Contract Upholstery

"Ovation" is another member of the
"Cordura Group." Also made with
Cordura nylon, it is puncture resistant,
flame retardant, fade resistant, will not
pill, and is treated with DuPont Teflon
soil and stain repellent.

Baby Gras Art Studio

Sao Paulo, Brazil

DESIGNER
Barbara "Baby" Gras, Principal
DESIGN FIRM
Baby Gras Art Studio

Barbara "Baby" Gras started her art studio in 1979—printing handmade fabrics, creating sculpture, painting with oils and designing custom jewelry.

In 1985, she started designing textiles for many manufacturers, following their specifications, to be utilized in home fashion and decoration.

In 1990, Baby Gras launched her first home decoration fabric collection.

Her textile designs have been highly acclaimed, and she has won many prizes and has been part of many exhibitions.

She received her design education at various colleges and universities in Brazil, France and the United States.

TEXTILE
"Fishes"
"Antares"
"Renovation"
"Renovation Composition"
MANUFACTURER
Baby Gras
USAGE
Home Furnishings
PHOTOGRAPHER
Tutu Cardoso de Almeida

Four different textile designs using varying colorways and patterns are shown here. Yet, the similarity in design makes these textiles work well together as complements in any interior setting.

TEXTILE
"Cotton Canvas"
DESIGNER
Baby Gras
USAGE
Home Furnishings
PHOTOGRAPHER
Tutu Cardoso de Almeida

An earthtone colorway of gold, rust, brown and beige combined with a highly-stylized geometric pattern forms a beautiful decorative textile.

TEXTILE
"Antares"
DESIGNER
Baby Gras
MANUFACTURER
Baby Gras
USAGE
Home Furnishings
PHOTOGRAPHER
Tutu Cardoso de Almeida

Stylized geometric forms in various colors and swirls of blue give dramatic impact to this design. The durability of the 100 percent cotton canvas makes this textile suitable for a variety of home furnishings.

TEXTILE
"Solo"
DESIGNER
Baby Gras
USAGE
Home Furnishings
PHOTOGRAPHER
Tutu Cardoso de Almeida

A vivid colorway and alternating geometric patterns create a current design that fits into many style interiors.

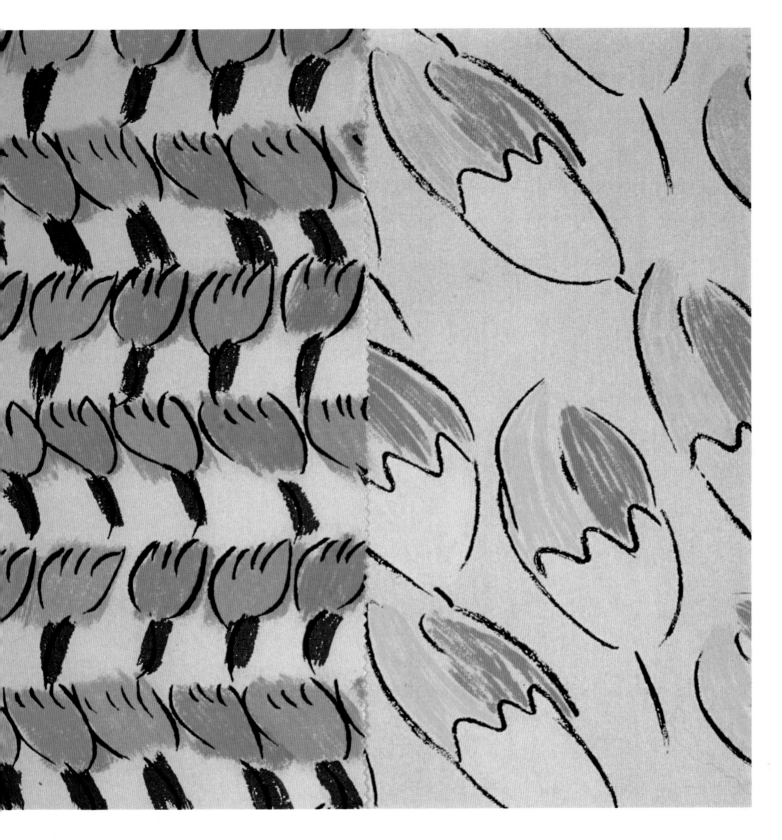

TEXTILE
"Flowers"
DESIGNER
Baby Gras
MANUFACTURER
Status Tecidos Ltda.
USAGE
Home Furnishings
PHOTOGRAPHER
Tutu Cardoso de Almeida

A vibrant mix of orange, yellow, green
and pink is the colorway for this
upholstery fabric. The textile is
constructed of 100 percent cotton
canvas, and is durable for any home
decorative use.

Naomi Lind Boccio

New York, New York

DESIGNER
Naomi Lind Boccio
DESIGN FIRM
Naomi Lind Boccio Designs

Naomi Lind Boccio is a New York-based textile designer and illustrator who specializes in designs for children. Her designs are used for children's home furnishings, garments, wallpapers, cloth storybooks, and cloth craft projects.

TEXTILE
"Silhouette Scene"
DESIGNER
Naomi Lind Boccio
DESIGN FIRM
Naomi Lind Boccio Designs
PHOTOGRAPHER
Van Cromes

This textile design, "Silhouette Scene," is intended for use on a bedspread.

TEXTILE
"Handcut Silhouettes"
DESIGNER
Naomi Lind Boccio
DESIGN FIRM
Naomi Lind Boccio Designs
PHOTOGRAPHER
Van Cromes

"Handcut Silhouettes" is a design for textiles to be utilized on children's bedspreads.

Chia Jen Studio

Scotia, California

DESIGNER
Jennifer Mackey
DESIGN FIRM
Chia Jen Studio

Chia Jen's hand-painted natural fibers are contemporary and refreshing. Jennifer Mackey, designer for Chia Jen, uses silks, cottons, and linens for her designs, which often evoke a Japanese mood. The majority of Chia Jen's custom work is in table top linens, floor canvasses, pillows, and drapery fabrics.

Jennifer Mackey studied throughout the U.S. and Europe. Her work has been represented in several national publications, galleries, and specialty stores.

TEXTILE/PRODUCT
"Blouse"
DESIGNER
Jennifer Mackey
DESIGN FIRM
Chia Jen
PHOTOGRAPHER
Walter Jebbe, Patrick Cudahy Studios

This blouse is a one-of-a-kind garment made with screen-printed, hand-painted, brushed and sponged crepe de chine.

TEXTILE/PRODUCT
"Series of Table Linens"
DESIGNER
Jennifer Mackey
DESIGN FIRM
Chia Jen
PHOTOGRAPHER
Walter Jebbe, Patrick Cudahy Studios

The three table linen designs shown
here show the versatility and technical
abilities of Jennifer Mackey for Chia
Jen. Each is hand-painted/printed,
rolled, and sponged.

TEXTILE/PRODUCT
"Pillows"
DESIGNER
Jennifer Mackey
DESIGN FIRM
Chia Jen
PHOTOGRAPHER
Walter Jebbe, Patrick Cudahy Studios

Mono-printed silk crepe de chine is
inset into raw silk in these pillows
designed by Jennifer Mackey for Chia
Jen. Each one measures 18"x18".

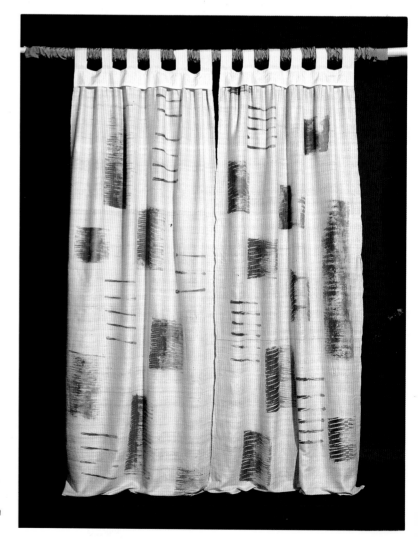

TEXTILE/PRODUCT
"Silk Draperies"
DESIGNER
Jennifer Mackey
DESIGN FIRM
Chia Jen
PHOTOGRAPHER
Walter Jebbe, Patrick Cudahy Studios

These draperies are hand-printed on
silk by Jennifer Mackey for Chia Jen.

TEXTILE/PRODUCT
"Series of Table Linens"
DESIGNER
Jennifer Mackey
DESIGN FIRM
Chia Jen
PHOTOGRAPHER
Walter Jebbe, Patrick Cudahy Studios

Christopher Hyland Inc.

New York, New York

Christopher Hyland, President of Christopher Hyland Incorporated located at 979 Third Avenue, New York City (tel. (212) 688-6121) is a fabric, trimmings, and wallpaper impressario. With a collection consisting of approximately thirteen thousand stock shopkeeping units, his firm is one of the most exciting sources for these items in the world. Custom possibilities are limitless. He believes that at the end of this century we are entering a period best described as Historic Design. This milieu consists of the juxtaposition of all types of historic design elements intermingled with the last one hundred years of outstanding modern design, whether building materials, furnishings, or art. He has over forty books containing his fabrics and other products available for purchase to design professionals.

TEXTILE
Various Designs
IMPRESSARIO
Christopher Hyland Incorporated
PHOTOGRAPHER
Steve Tague

This photograph vividly and beautifully portrays numerous applications of a variety of textiles, usually utilized in home furnishings. On mannequin: jacket—"Van der Weyden"; skirt— "Royal Windsor Velvet"; fabric at neck—"Classical Star"; suit jacket (left)—"Damasco Giudecca"; suit jacket (right)—"Lame Damask"; blouse (right)—"Taffeta"; fabric swag (right)—"La Diva Damask"; fabric behind swag—"Crespi"; tufted ottoman—"Brussels Velvet"; wall covering—"Patricia's Sun Fabric."

TEXTILE
"Animal Heaven"
DESIGNER
Celia Birtwell
IMPRESSARIO
Christopher Hyland Incorporated
PHOTOGRAPHER
Steve Tague

"Animal Heaven" is a 100 percent silk organza in gold on white. The design is an adaptation of a 17th-century embroidery from the Victoria and Albert Museum. The lower curtain fabric, titled "Classical Star," is also 100 percent silk organza. The wall covering, "Patricia's Sun Fabric," is 100 percent silk duppion. The design is a collaboration between Gilbert Lesser, Artistic Director of LIFE magazine, and Christopher Hyland. The inspiration for this textile was provided both by Mr. Hyland's mothers' 19th-century sun brooch and the sun above the door of the city palace of the Maharajah of Jaipur.

TEXTILE
"Memlinc"
IMPRESSARIO
Christopher Hyland Incorporated
PHOTOGRAPHER
Steve Tague

"Memlinc" is a 50 percent cotton, 50 percent silk blend utilized for home furnishings. The fabric is a medieval design in a lichen/fawn colorway and is coordinated with "Dufour" wallpaper. "Striped Taffeta" is used for the lining.

TEXTILE
"Palatino"
DESIGNER
Helge Stussel
IMPRESSARIO
Christopher Hyland Incorporated
PHOTOGRAPHER
Steve Tague

"Palatino" is a blend of viscose (77 percent), silk (20 percent), and cotton (3 percent).

TEXTILE
"Willow"
IMPRESSARIO
Christopher Hyland Incorporated

"Willow" is a 100 percent cotton chintz inspired by a 19th-century porcelain pattern.

TEXTILE
"Tai Pan Damask"
IMPRESSARIO
Christopher Hyland Incorporated
PHOTOGRAPHER
Steve Tague

"Tai Pan Damask" is a silk (40 percent) and viscose (60 percent) blend. The lining is 100 percent silk—"Shot Taffeta." The coordinating wall covering, "Versailles," was designed by Christopher Hyland and is shown here in gold on a green/blue stripe.

TEXTILE
"Clara Completo"
IMPRESSARIO
Christopher Hyland Incorporated
PHOTOGRAPHER
Steve Tague

"Clara Completo" is composed of 100 percent Panama cotton in a white, blue, light blue and yellow colorway. The design is of a Hispano-Portuguese-Tyrolian origin. The lining, "Clara's Bouquet," is also of 100 percent Panama cotton. The coordinating wall covering, "Nimue," is a white on yellow colorway based on a late 18th-century historic document.

TEXTILE
"Laurel"
IMPRESSARIO
Christopher Hyland Incorporated
PHOTOGRAPHER
Steve Tague

"Laurel" is a 30 percent silk and 70 percent cotton blend in a green colorway based on an historic Venetian design. The lining, "Trellis Moire," is done in a silk (30 percent) and viscose (70 percent) blend based on an historic Italian design. The coordinating wallpaper, "Trellis," is gold on a redwood stripe and based on an early 19th-century design by Pugin.

TEXTILE
"Fleur de Lys"
IMPRESSARIO
Christopher Hyland Incorporated
PHOTOGRAPHER
Steve Tague

"Fleur de Lys" is a 100 percent cotton fabric based on an historic Victorian design produced in a red and yellow colorway. "Hertford Stripe," a 100 percent cotton chintz, is used for the lining.

TEXTILE
"Magellan"
DESIGNER
Gamme
IMPRESSARIO
Christopher Hyland Incorporated
PHOTOGRAPHER
Steve Tague

"Magellan" is 100 percent silk and is lined with "Tintoretto," also in 100 percent silk. "Florentine Lily," the coordinating wallpaper, is gold on light blue and is based on an historic Florentine design.

TEXTILE
"Wood Anemone"
DESIGNER
Glynn Boyd Harte
IMPRESSARIO
Christopher Hyland Incorporated
PHOTOGRAPHER
Steve Tague

"Wood Anemone" is 100 percent cotton in a pink stripe. The lining, done in a blueberry colorway in 100 percent cotton, is titled "Cotton Check."

Cinnabar Traders

New York, New York

DESIGNER
Karen Hudson
DESIGN FIRM
Cinnabar Traders, Ltd.

Karen Hudson is Vice President and Creative Director of Cinnabar Traders Ltd., a textile converter of wovens and prints and an apparel manufacturer of men's and women's sportswear.

Prior to joining Cinnabar, Karen Hudson was a costume stylist and art teacher. She is married and has two children.

TEXTILE
"Haberdashery"
DESIGNER
Karen Hudson
CLIENT/MFR
Ruff Hewn

"Haberdashery" is a design created as part of a line with an equestrian theme. It is 100 percent cotton twill, screen-printed in Japan through Marubeni.

TEXTILE
"Indian Arrowheads"
DESIGNER
Karen Hudson
CLIENT/MFR
C.M.T. Enterprises

"Indian Arrowheads" is 100 percent brushed cotton twill, printed in Japan through Marubeni.

TEXTILE
"Undersea Batik"
DESIGNER
Karen Hudson
CLIENT/MFR
Perry Ellis

"Undersea Batik" was printed in Korea on cotton linen.

TEXTILE
"Hit the Deck"
DESIGNER
Karen Hudson
CLIENT/MFR
Ruff Hewn

"Hit the Deck" was designed with a 1940's motif as part of a collection based on a nautical theme. It is 100 percent cotton poplin, screen-printed in Japan through Marubeni.

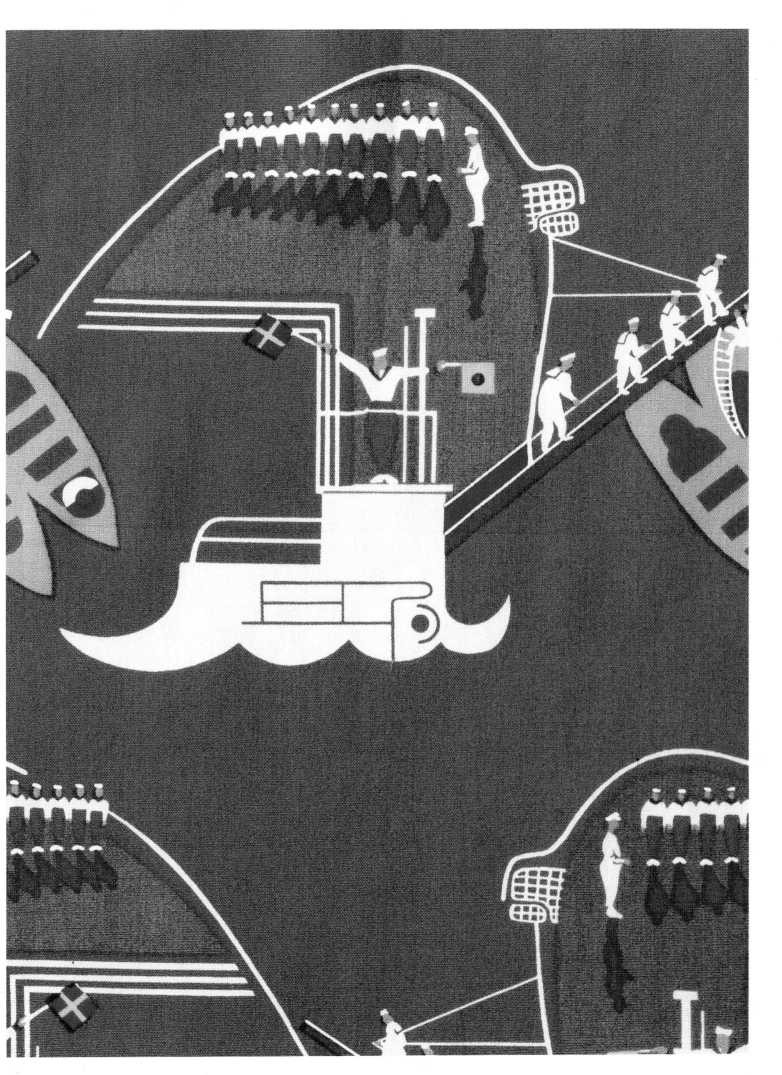

Clarence House

New York, New York

Clarence House is an international resource for fine furnishing fabrics, wallpapers and trimmings. Founded in 1961, Clarence House is headquartered in New York City with trade showrooms in every major U.S. market.

Under the chairmanship of founder Robin Roberts and Art Director Kazumi Yoshida, Clarence House creates designs based on documents from the 17th century through the early 20th century.

TEXTILE
"Gropius"
DESIGN FIRM
Clarence House
PHOTOGRAPHER
Bill McConnell

Woven in Italy, Gropius is inspired by the designs of the Bauhaus architect Walter Gropius. The classic Art Deco geometry is enhanced by the cut and uncut loop construction of the face. The backing of Gropius is a linen and cotton blend while the face is 100 percent linen. This design has been colored in three typical period combinations, dark blue, green and rose.

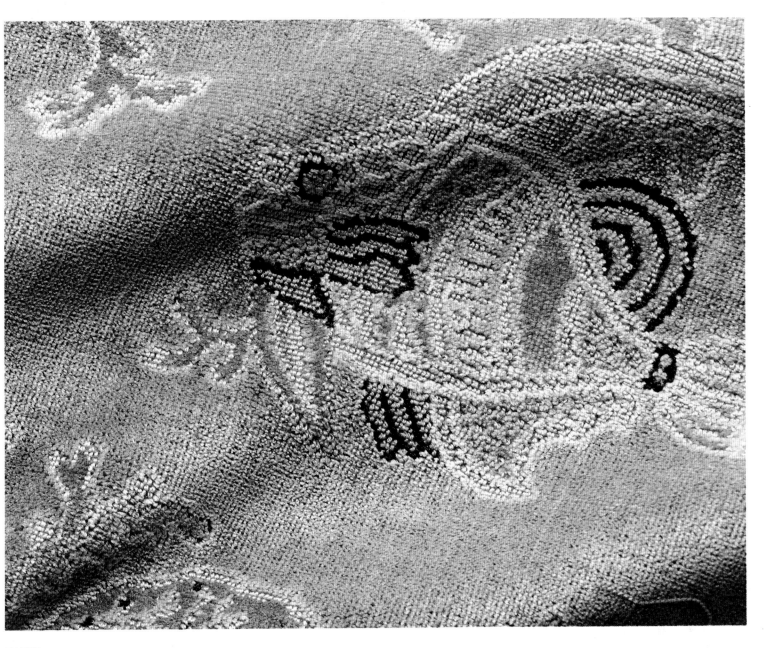

TEXTILE
"Poissonniere"
DESIGN FIRM
Clarence House
PHOTOGRAPHER
Bill McConnell

The document for this design was woven in Holland in the early 18th century for the King of Portugal. The original construction of an all silk cut and uncut loop face has been interpreted in linen flax and cotton. This design, now woven in France, incorporates all the motifs of the document in the original colorway.

TEXTILE
"Parade des Animaux"
DESIGN FIRM
Clarence House
PHOTOGRAPHER
Bill McConnell

Parade des Animaux pays homage to
and is inspired by the 20th-century
furniture designs of Diego Giacometti.
Woven in France as a cotton gros
point, this parade of highly stylized
animals is available in four colorways.

TEXTILE
"Damasco Borgia"
DESIGN FIRM
Clarence House
PHOTOGRAPHER
Bill McConnell

Based on an Italian Renaissance document, this design epitomizes the art of damask weaving. Grandly scaled and brilliantly colored, Damasco Borgia is woven of 100 percent silk in Belgium

TEXTILE
"Arts and Crafts"
DESIGN FIRM
Clarence House
PHOTOGRAPHER
Bill McConnell

Arts and Crafts in reproduced from a document in the Clarence House archive of an English drapery panel c. 1900. This design incorporates many of the derivative elements of this era; the combination of architectural elements (neo-gothic and neo-romanesque) and flat, two dimensional representations of nature. True to the document, Arts and Crafts is printed on 100 percent linen. Arts and Crafts is available in the original and two period colorways.

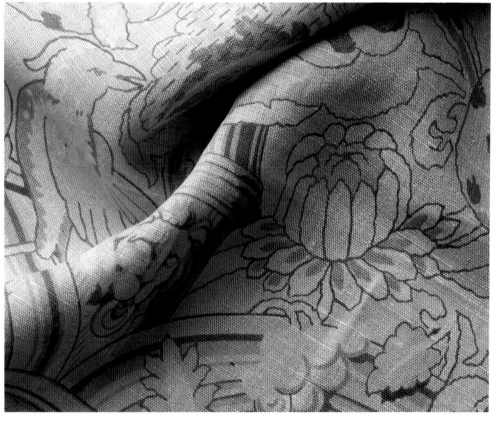

TEXTILE
"Madeleine"
DESIGN FIRM
Clarence House
PHOTOGRAPHER
Bill McConnell

Reproduced from an 18th-century French hand-painted silk document in the Clarence House archive, Madeleine is hand-screened in France. Originally painted in the Chinese manner, the top colors in this design maintain the same crisp, fresh feeling of the document. Clarence House has printed this design in two qualities, on an all cotton percale and on 100 percent glazed cotton in six colorways.

TEXTILE
"Botanica"
DESIGN FIRM
Clarence House
PHOTOGRAPHER
Bill McConnell

Printed by hand in Italy on 100 percent cotton percale, Botanica is a large scale (a 47⅝" repeat) thirty-two screen design. The document for this design is an 18th-century Chinese sketchbook of exotic flora. The available groundcolors, beige and taupe, mimic the original paper. The screen engraving here is exceptional; the subtle detailing of the flowers is almost life-like.

TEXTILE
"Grand Tableau Chinoise"
DESIGN FIRM
Clarence House
PHOTOGRAPHER
Bill McConnell

Inspired by a set of 18th century silk Chinoiserie panels from the Clarence House archive, this design is hand printed in Italy on 100% Egyptian long-staple cotton. Requiring great care and attention, two years were spent engraving the forty-eight screens that make this textile a superior technical achievement. This design is scaled to the document (a 48" repeat) and available in one period colorway only.

Conrad Imports

San Francisco, California

Conrad Imports' lines of wall coverings and window coverings are all handwoven in the Orient by master weavers. The products are made of natural reeds, grasses, and fibers.

TEXTILE/PRODUCT
Original Sunshades #AC241 (Tortoise Shell), #AC240 (Natural)
DESIGNER
Conrad Imports
PHOTOGRAPHY
Synapse, San Francisco

These unique, open weave shades allow filtered sun protection while preserving outside views. These custom handwoven window coverings are composed of select natural grasses, reeds and fibers.

TEXTILE/PRODUCT
Reed Weaves Sunshades #1431 (natural with white jute), #1404 (jade), #1411 (natural with natural jute)

DESIGNER
Conrad Imports
PHOTOGRAPHY
Synapse, San Francisco

Each sunshade is individually hand-woven and suitable for many styles of interiors. These sunshades are the winner of the ASID International Award.

TEXTILE/PRODUCT
"Conrad Original Sunshades-Weave #1209
(Suma Weave)"
Horizontal Installation in Kneedler-Fauchere
Showroom by Henry C. Ford
PHOTOGRAPHER
John Rogers, Dallas
FURNITURE
E.C. Dicken Showroom, Dallas

Handwoven wall covering of golden
wheat and natural jute come 9' wide
by 30 yards long without any seams.

TEXTILE/PRODUCT
"Conrad Original Sunshades-Weave #219"
"Conrad Suma Weave Wall Covering"
PHOTOGRAPHER
John Rogers, Dallas
FURNITURE
E.C. Dicken Showroom, Dallas

An interior utilizing Conrad's
handwoven sunshades and wall
covering.

TEXTILE/PRODUCT
"Conrad Original Sunshades-Weave #1"
PHOTOGRAPHER
John Rogers, Dallas

Winner of the ASID International Award. A subtle, handwoven window treatment. Each sunshade is individually handwoven with natural grasses, reeds and fibers.

Michael A. Cummings

New York, New York

Michael A. Cummings is a New York City-based designer and fine artist who creates quilts and T-shirt designs with bright colors, exciting patterns, and evocative imagery. His works have been exhibited at numerous museums and galleries and can be found in corporate, private, and museum collections. His textile designs have been used in advertisements for Kodak, and articles about his work have appeared in the New York Times, Washington Post, and other publications. He designed and implemented art cirriculum for 800 elementary school children and taught art at a New York City public school.

TEXTILE/PRODUCT
"African Jazz Series #1"
"African Jazz Series #2"
ARTIST/DESIGNER
Michael A. Cummings
MANUFACTURER
Connie Blumberg
PHOTOGRAPHER
Sarah Wells, New York

These two quilts, measuring 72" x 96" each, are from a series of 12. The designs were created after seeing a poster showing three African musicians playing jazz in a cafe. Artistic references such as Romare Bearden, Rousseau, and Egungun costumes found in the Yoruba society of Western Nigeria and Eastern Dahomey were influences in the "African Jazz" series.

TEXTILE/PRODUCT
"T-shirt Designs"
DESIGNER
Michael A. Cummings
MANUFACTURER
Print Workshop Inc., NYC
USAGE
T-shirts
PHOTOGRAPHER
Michael A. Cummings

These "T-shirt Designs" are printed in black and white and then hand colored.

TEXTILE/PRODUCT
"Haitian Boat People #1"
"Haitian Boat People #2"
ARTIST/DESIGNER
Michael A. Cummings
PHOTOGRAPHER
Sarah Wells, New York

This wall hanging series was developed after exposure to media reports on the Haitian Boat People attempting to escape from their island. These quilts measure 72" x 96".

59

Kurt Delbanco

New York, New York

Kurt Delbanco's activities in the visual arts began during his childhood in Hamburg, Germany. He studied fine arts in Europe and the U.S. and has been associated with many notables in the art world. His paintings, sculptures, product designs, textile designs, and home furnishing designs are in numerous public and private collections.

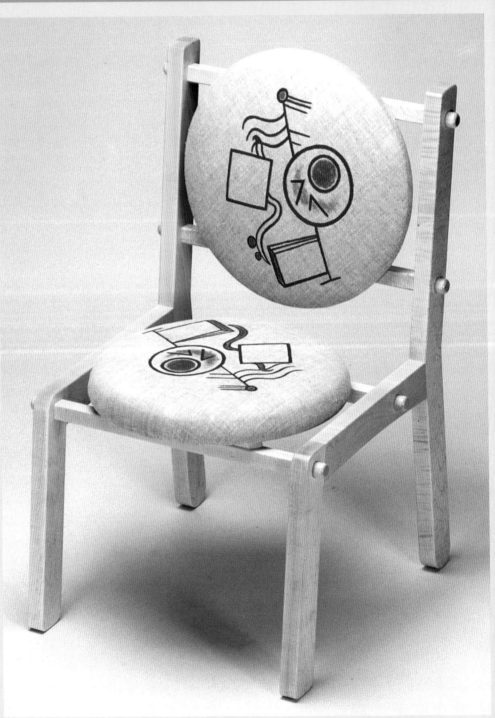

TEXTILE/PRODUCT
"Delbanco Chairs"
DESIGNER
Kurt Delbanco

Kurt Delbamco's textile design as applied to a variety of seating: chairs for one, two, and three occupants. His textile designs are examples of his philosophy of "changeability."

Design on Fabric

Champaign, Illinois

DESIGNER
Katharine Parham, Co-Owner
DESIGN FIRM
Design on Fabric

Katharine Parham lives in Illinois and has been painting on fabric for over seven years. The work of her company, Design on Fabric (which she co-owns with Ellen S. Parham), is sold in galleries in Illinois, Maryland, Rhode Island, and Tennessee. Three of Parham's scarves were exhibited in Craft Media I: The Artist's Perspective, a national show held at Northern Illinois University in 1989.

TEXTILE
"Cotton"
USAGE
Fashion Accessory
PHOTOGRAPHER
Keith Hill

Red, yellow, blue, purple and green Deka fabric paint was used on this 20" x 20" cotton scarf.

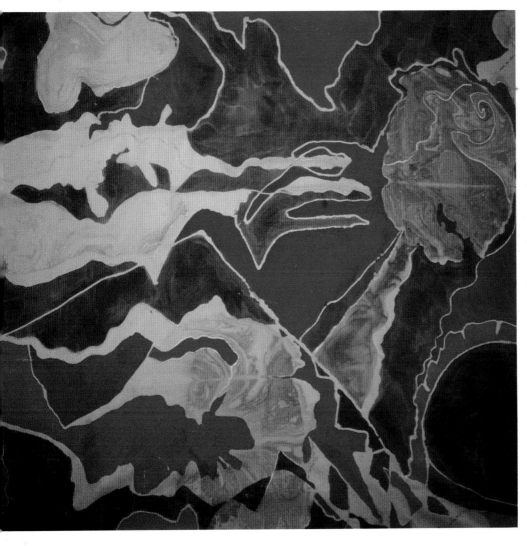

TEXTILE
"Crepe de Chine"
USAGE
Fashion Accessory
PHOTOGRAPHER
Craig Fischer

The color scheme used incorporates
shades of purple and red with
touches of yellow and gold. A
DekaSilk fabric paint, with clear, water-
soluble resist, gold resist and
marblizing medium was used on a
35" x 35" 12 momme crepe de chine.

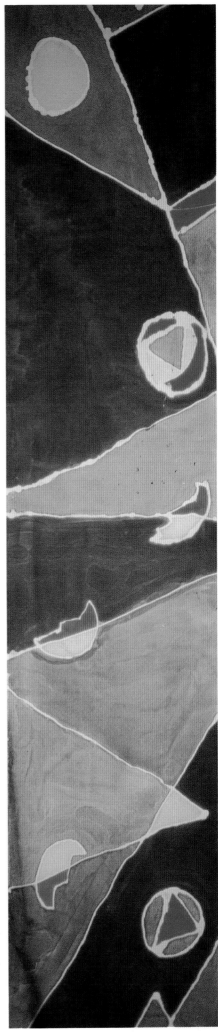

TEXTILE
"Crepe de Chine"
USAGE
Fashion Accessory
PHOTOGRAPHER
Craig Fischer

This silk 12 momme crepe de chine
scarf contains a pattern done in blue,
green, yellow and red. DekaSilk fabric
paint with clear resist was used on this
12" x 70" piece.

TEXTILE
"Shantung Silk"
USAGE
Fashion Accessory
PHOTOGRAPHER
Illini Studio

This black, blue, yellow and white
design was executed using Deka
Fabric paint on a 30" x 30" square of
red silk shantung.

TEXTILE
"Cotton"
USAGE
Fashion Accessory
PHOTOGRAPHER
Keith Hill

An unusual design, reminiscent of
flowers, is done in a color scheme of
purple, blue and green. Deka fabric
paint was used.

Donghia

New York, New York

Sherri Donghia
Vice President of Design Marketing/
Sales for Donghia Furniture/Textiles

A former fashion industry professional, Ms. Donghia has successfully forayed her marketing and sales expertise into the furniture and textile industry.

Ms. Donghia's background includes executive positions with Bloomingdale's, Gimbels, and Federated Department Stores. She also opened her own consulting firm where she provided a number of merchandising concepts for clients such as the Rockresort Hotels, Paul Costello's Women's Collection, and Alexander Julian.

Ms. Donghia came to work for the company founded by her cousin, the late Angelo Donghia, in 1987.

Donghia Furniture/Textiles grew out of Angelo Donghia's first product company, And Vice Versa, founded in 1968. His philosophy, maintained and encouraged today, was that nothing should carry the Donghia name unless it was a consistent evolution of the Donghia Style, promoted design integrity, and maintained superior production values.

Donghia's elegant textile designs reflect a wide range of influences: handwoven textures of India, Matisse collages, Renaissance heraldry, and many more. An unusual sense of texture and unique color sensibility are Donghia's hallmarks.

TEXTILE
"Lightning Bolt"
DESIGNER
Beverly Thome
DESIGN FIRM
Donghia
PHOTOGRAPHER
Robert Grant

This zigzag stripe fabric features three alternating colors enhanced by bolts of contrasting tones. The matelasse effect is created by the double warp construction. The textile is composed of linen, cotton and polyester that produces an iridescent quality. The fabric is 54" wide with a 4½" vertical repeat and a 3½" horizontal repeat.

TEXTILE
"Khyber"
DESIGNER
Glenn Peckman
DESIGN FIRM
Donghia
PHOTOGRAPHER
Robert Grant

A blend of cross-cultural design
images influenced by American Indian
blanketry and African hand-loomed
textiles, "Khyber," designed by Glenn
Peckman, is of plush woven velvet, in
six colorways.
Textile designer Glenn Peckman was
originally a painter. His extensive
travels offer exposure to other periods
and cultures which inspire his
contemporary textiles.

TEXTILE
"Savoy Stripe"
DESIGNER
Glenn Peckman
DESIGN FIRM
Donghia
USAGE
Upholstery, Draperies

Glenn Peckman's design for Donghia, "Savoy Stripe, is an opulent print with subtle depth and striking textural effects. Woven of 100 percent cotton sateen, "Savoy Stripe" is available in a palette that ranges from pale neutral to rich dark hues. It comes in a 50.5" width with a 6.25" repeat.

TEXTILE
"Palio" and "Regatta"
DESIGNER
John Hutton
DESIGN FIRM
Donghia
PHOTOGRAPHERS
Frank Lindler, Jeff Goldberg

The regal, overscaled designs of "Palio" and "Regatta" convey a dramatic, graphic message. Woven in Europe, these textiles are 100 percent wool damask. "Regatta" features an undulating, serpentine pattern. "Palio" is a pattern of elongated diamond shapes.
John Hutton, Design Director for Donghia Furniture creates designs based on his study of classic proportion. He has been associated with Donghia since the 1970's.

TEXTILE
"Arras"
DESIGNER
Glenn Peckman
DESIGN FIRM
Donghia
CHAIR
"Plaza Suite"/Donghia Furniture
PHOTOGRAPHER
Kelly Campbell

"Arras" is a woven tapestry of 94 percent cotton and 6 percent viscose, reminiscent of traditional Renaissance tapestries. "Arras" blends a modern geometric pattern with heraldic crests in deep tapestry colors and is available in three colorways, rouge, verte, and bleue.

TEXTILE
"New Ways"
DESIGNER
Richard Giglio
DESIGN FIRM
Donghia
PHOTOGRAPHER
Don Freeman

"New Ways" is a collection of four textile designs based on the paintings, drawings and collages of artist/designer Richard Giglio. "Figures" reflects the strong influence of Giglio's collages. It evokes motifs from Japan, or Africa, or even the look of pony skin. "Selloum", a sea of lines floating freely across the fabric, illustrates the artist's spontaneous dialogue with space. "Palms" echoes the leafy forms and windswept movement of tropical palm trees. "Eaton Squares" is a smaller-scaled, hand-drawn geometric companion print to the entire collection. "New Ways" is printed on 100 percent cotton pebblecloth.

The Fabric Workshop
Philadelphia, Pennsylvania

The Fabric Workshop is the only non-profit organization in the U.S. devoted to experimental fabric design and printing by emerging and nationally recognized artists representing all disciplines. Founded in 1977, The Fabric Workshop has developed into a renowned institution with a nationally recognized Artist-in Residence program, an extensive permanent museum collection of unique and exciting artworks, and comprehensive educational programming including exhibitions, lectures, tours and student apprenticeships.

Marion Boulton Stroud is Founder and Artistic Director of the Fabric Workshop. A graduate of the University of Pennsylvania (B.A. 1961, M.A. 1969), Stroud attended the Harvard Business School Arts Administration Program. She serves on committees for both the Philadelphia Museum of Art and The Whitney Museum of Art.

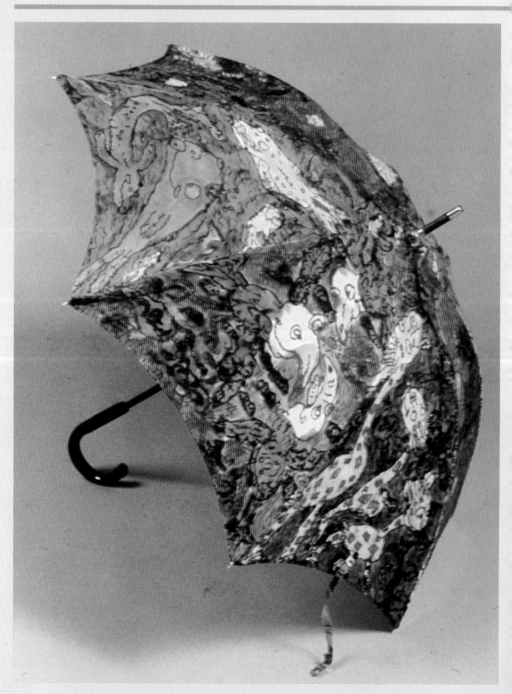

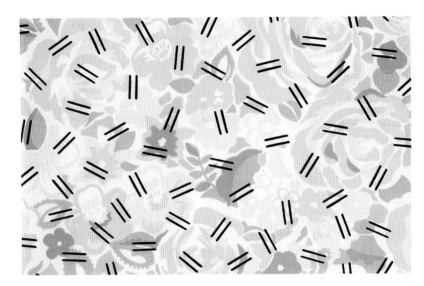

TEXTILE
"Grandmother"
DESIGNER
Robert Venturi

TEXTILE/PRODUCT
"Notebook and Grandmother"
DESIGNER
Robert Venturi

TEXTILE/PRODUCT
"Gingko Kimono"
DESIGNER
Diane Itter

TEXTILE/PRODUCT
"Best Foot Forward"
DESIGNER
Jame Carpenter

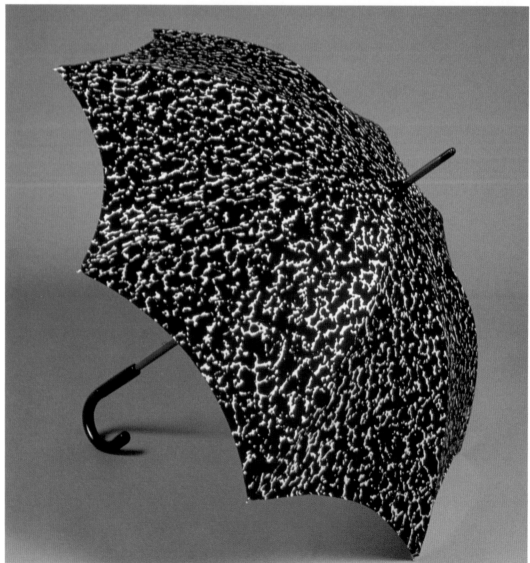

TEXTILE/PRODUCT
"Notebook Umbrella"
DESIGNER
Robert Venturi

TEXTILE/PRODUCT
"Hidden Bag"
DESIGNER
Will Stokes, Jr.

TEXTILE/PRODUCT
"Gridley Bag"
DESIGNER
Roy Deforest

TEXTILE/PRODUCT
"Hawaiian Punch"
DESIGNER
Robert Kushner

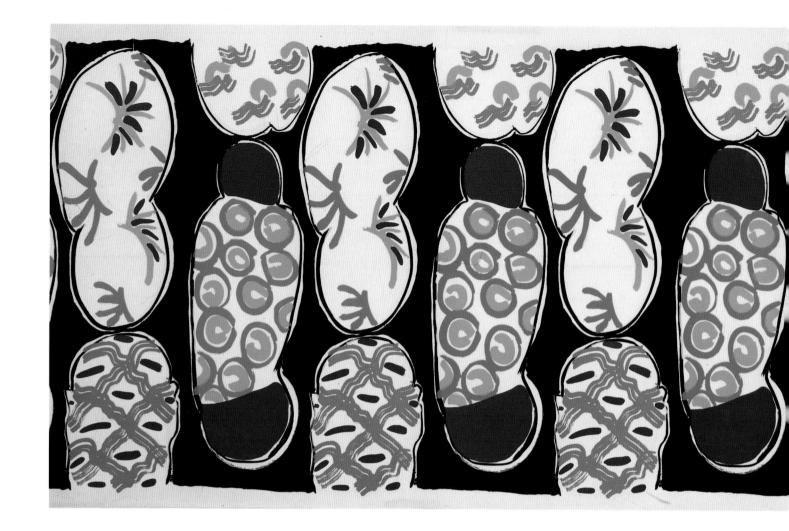

TEXTILE
"Platters"
DESIGNER
Betty Woodman

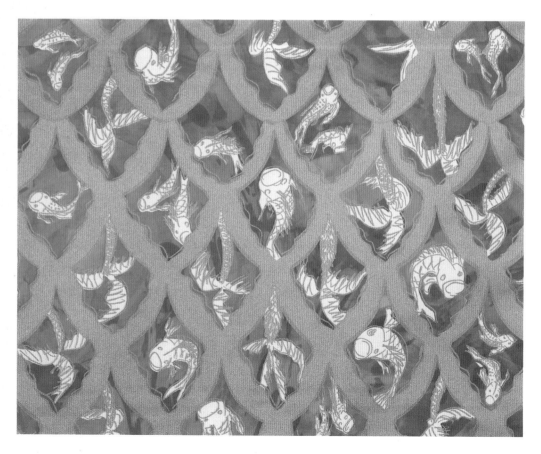

TEXTILE
"Pattern Palm"
DESIGNER
Ned Smyth

TEXTILE
"Dinner"
DESIGNER
John Moore

TEXTILE
"Hidden"
DESIGNER
Will Stokes, Jr.

TEXTILE/PRODUCT
"Lino Tile" Chair
DESIGNER
Tony Costanzo

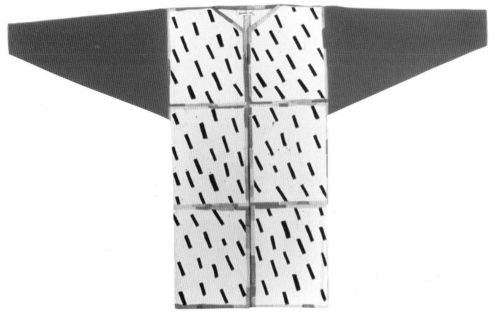

TEXTILE/PRODUCT
"Coat"
DESIGNER
Jun Kaneko

TEXTILE/PRODUCT
"Shirt"
DESIGNER
Jun Kaneko

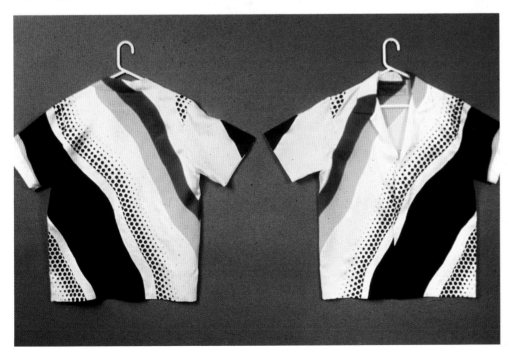

TEXTILE/PRODUCT
"Shirt"
DESIGNER
Roy Lichtenstein

TEXTILE/PRODUCT
"Open Window Curtain"
DESIGNER
Scott Burton

Harlem Textile Works

New York, New York

Harlem Textile Works is a program of the Children's Art Carnival, a non-profit art school dedicated to the creative development of youth ages 4 - 21. Founded in 1984, Harlem Textile Works designs, manufactures, and sells hand-screened decorative fabrics, home textiles, and accessories, with earnings benefitting Harlem Textile Works and Children's Art Carnival programs. Ms. Kerris Wolsky serves as director and head designer for this program.

TEXTILE
"Kente"
DESIGNER
Kerris Wolsky
TEXTILE
"Clown"
DESIGNER
Children's Art Carnival
TEXTILE
"Mudcloth"
DESIGNER
Zahiyya Abdul-Karim
(Harlem Textile Works Intern, Age 17)
TEXTILE
"Freedom"
DESIGNER
Jose Ortiz
(Children's Art Carnival Student, Age 14)
TEXTILE
"Plate"
DESIGNER
Kerris Wolsky
USAGE
T-shirts
MANUFACTURER
Harlem Textile Works, NY, NY
PHOTOGRAPHER
Dawoud Bey

This collection of cotton T-shirts is hand-screened with a variety of exciting textile designs.

TEXTILE
"Cote de Shell", "Abidjahn", "Spiral Maze",
"Madagascar Lily"
DESIGNER
J. Michelle Hill
Designs based on original children's
artwork
USAGE
Multiple
MANUFACTURER
Harlem Textile Works, NY, NY
PHOTOGRAPHER
Dawoud Bey

These organic patterns, hand-
screened on cotton fabrics, were
suggested by children's original
artwork. The textiles' simple beauty
makes them suitable for a variety of
applications.

TEXTILE
"Ipanema"
DESIGNER
J. Michelle Hill
TEXTILE
"Bold Cut-Outs"
DESIGNER
Betty Blayton-Taylor
TEXTILE
"Temmi"
DESIGNER
J. Michelle Hills
TEXTILE
"Kasai"
DESIGNER
Kerris Wolsky
USAGE
Multiple
MANUFACTURER
Harlem Textile Works, NY, NY
PHOTOGRAPHER
Dawoud Bey

This bold variety of hand-screened
cotton fabrics has an earthy and exotic
appeal.

TEXTILE
"Zahiyya"
DESIGNER
Zahiyya Abdul-Karim
TEXTILE
"Mali"
DESIGNER
Kerris Wolsky
TEXTILE
"Mudcloth I"
DESIGNER
J. Michelle Hill
TEXTILE
"Mudcloth II"
DESIGNER
J. Michelle Hill
USAGE
Multiple
MANUFACTURER
Harlem Textile Works, NY, NY
PHOTOGRAPHER
Dawoud Bey

These black-and-white patterns, some
of which were adapted from African
Mudcloth fabrics, are hand-screened
on cotton fabrics.

J.M. Lynne

Rifton, New York

J.M. Lynne designs wallcoverings using natural fiber linen and linen blend woven textiles in a broad range of subtle designs.

Michael Landsberg, executive vice president of the twenty-seven-year-old J.M. Lynne Company, Inc. and president of their eight-year-old subsidiary, Adam James Textiles, Inc., works closely with their in-house design team to produce wallcoverings and fabric upholstery based on the demands of interior designers and specifiers.

TEXTILE
"Striations"
DESIGNER
J.M. Lynne
DESIGN FIRM
J.M. Lynne Wallcovering
USAGE
Wallcovering

"Striations" is a high density contract wallcovering collection for use in high-traffic areas. Vertical "string" characteristics inherent in the collection allow for a subtle three-dimensional effect. Warp lays in the "Striations" collection are treated with a special water-resistant coating that promotes washability.

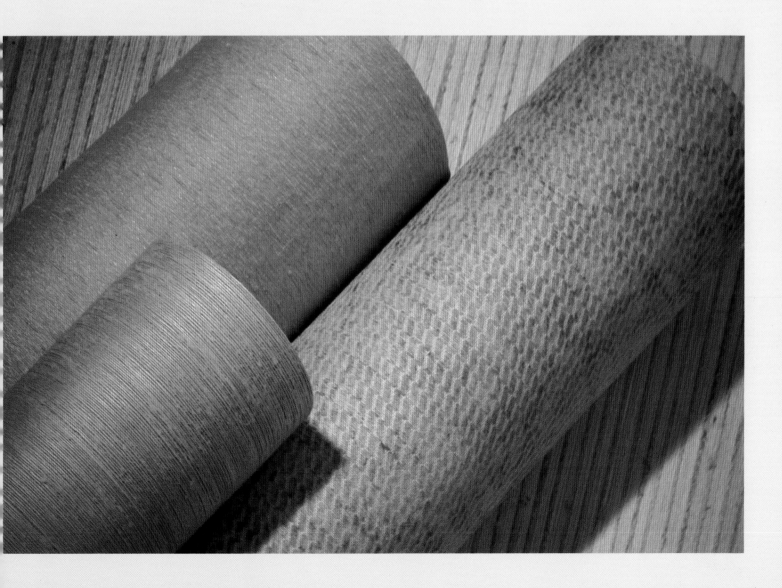

TEXTILE
"Harbour Designs"
DESIGNER
J.M. Lynne
DESIGN FIRM
J.M. Lynne Wallcovering
USAGE
Wallcovering

"Harbour Designs" is an attractive
wallcovering textile with a subtle mix
of multicolor, solid color and neutral
colors. Sixty-one patterns and
colorings in the collection create
neutral, pastel, and mid-tone effects
on office walls.

Jane-Albert Studio Inc.

New York, New York

arola Amsinck graduated with a Diploma
Industrial Design from the "Hochschule
r Bildende Kuenste" in Hamburg, Ger-
any.

efore coming to New York in 1983, she
on a competition for designing curtains.
addition, she has designed a signature
ollection of silk pillows and a wallpaper
ollection.

America, she has designed for all areas
surface design: from infant products
d papergoods to home furnishings and
ramic tiles. She styles for home product
mpanies and publishes an annual trend
port.

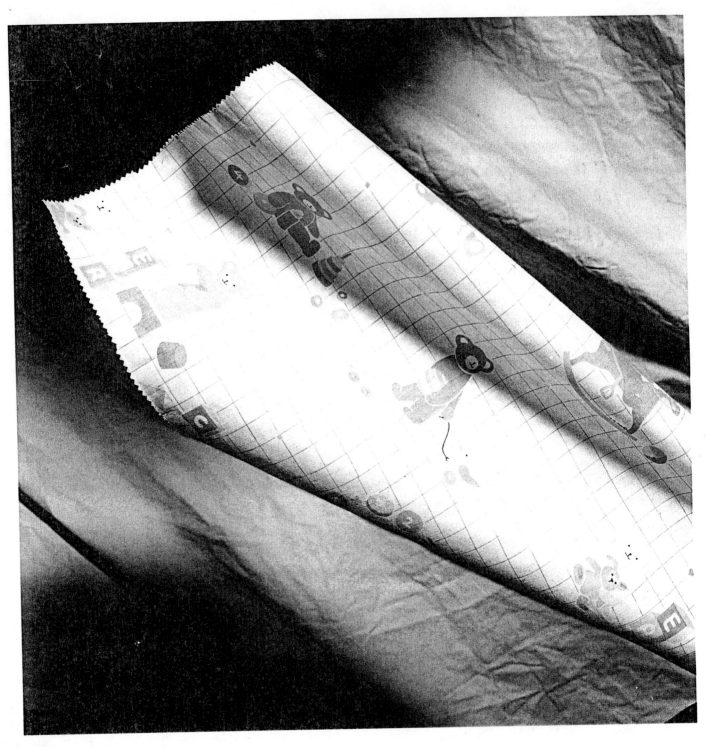

PRODUCT
"Baby Bears" and "Carola's Bears"
© C. Amsinck 1986, marketed under "Baby
Bears" and "Carola's Bears" logos.
MANUFACTURERS
Bedding—Curity®
Soft Care Apparel—Curity®
DESIGNER
Carola Amsinck

A pastel colorway and soft background adds graphic appeal to this
bear-patterned textile created
exclusively for the baby market.

Libby Kowalski

New York, New York

DESIGN FIRM
CTD Studio

Designer Libby Kowalski received her M.F.A. from Cranbrook Academy of Art. Since then she has created a national and international name for herself as a fiber Artist. She is a professor in the Fine Arts Department at SUNY Cortland and also the designer/owner of the CTD studio in Manhattan.

Libby Kowalski's CTD Studio is a well-known handloom and woven design studio which is highly computerized. CTD Studio allows Kowalski to work with clients in all facets of the textile industry in a variety of ways. CTD is also a handloom prototype studio.

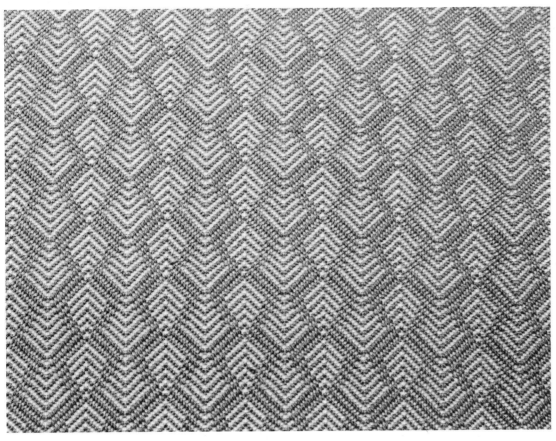

TEXTILES
"CTD Studio Portfolio Textiles"
DESIGNER
Libby Kowalski
DESIGN FIRM
CTD Studio
PHOTOGRAPHER
John Reis

These varied examples of CTD's freelance portfolio of textile designs are woven from cotton yarns and meet the construction and structural constraints of the contract upholstery/wallcovering market. They were designed with the aid of the CADET Textile Design system, which is a very sophisticated computer-aided design system.

TEXTILES
"CTD Studio Portfolio Textiles"
DESIGNER
Libby Kowalski
DESIGN FIRM
CTD Studio
PHOTOGRAPHER
John Reis

Knoll Textiles

New York, New York

DESIGNER
Peter Eisenman

Peter Eisenman is an architect and educator of international acclaim. His work with Knoll Textiles consists of architecturally inspired unpholstery fabrics based on award-winning building designs by Eisenman.

TEXTILE
The "Snakes and Ladders" Collection
© The Knoll Group, 1990
DESIGNER
Peter Eisenman for Knoll Textiles
USAGE
Upholstery

The "Snakes and Ladders" collection consists of five fabrics, all of woven wool.

DESIGNER
Jhane Barnes

TEXTILE
The "Nature" Collection
© The Knoll Group, 1990
DESIGNER
Jhane Barnes for Knoll Textiles
USAGE
Upholstery and Panel

Jhane Barnes is acknowledged as both a modernist pioneer of American apparel and a visionary of textile design. She won her first COTY for menswear in 1980, and in 1984 won the COTY Return Menswear Award. In addition, she is being honored as the first recipient of the Dalmore Design Review, recognizing a designer's contribution to the way American businessmen dress.

Jhane Barnes, Inc. has evolved to meet the international demands for her design expertise through various licensing agreements, including that with the Knoll Group for contract textiles.

The "Nature" Collection by Jhane Barnes is a line of coordinating panel and upholstery fabrics. The panel fabrics are blends of wool, cotton, nylon, and polyester, as are the upholstery fabrics.

Jack Lenor Larsen

New York, New York

Jack Lenor Larsen Incorporated, founded in 1953 by its namesake, is today a dominant force in international fabrics and a major influence on environmental design. "The Larsen look" began with handwoven fabrics of varied yarns in random repeats. Many of these won design awards. The years since read like a who's who of important commissions and works selected for the permanent collections of major museums. Larsen Design Studio mentors include such masters as William Morris, Mariano Fortuny, and Louis C. Tiffany—as well as the weavers of ancient and tribal traditions. Like the Larsen team, they looked to evolving needs, created within new and old technologies, and sustained quality and style. "Our prints," Larsen says, "are not applied graphics, but a handicraft expressing the marriage of the thirsty cloth and liquid dye."

As Jack Larsen is a scholar, author and traveler, many of his collections derive from a culture or a people; others have grown out of his involvement with new or old technologies. These many developments over the years include the first printed velvets in 1959 and the first stretch upholsteries in 1961. Larsen Carpet and Larsen Leather in 1976. Today the Larsen organization, under the firm leadership of its President, Pat Lembo, is global with production centers in 30 countries and Larsen showrooms in as many major cities around the world.

TEXTILE
"Imperial Silk"
DESIGN FIRM
Jack Lenor Larsen

"Imperial Silk," a silken double-cloth, was designed for drapery applications.

TEXTILE
"Grail Silk"
DESIGN FIRM
Jack Lenor Larsen

"Grail Silk" is a textured silk textile design suitable for multiple uses.

TEXTILE
"Pegasus"
DESIGN FIRM
Jack Lenor Larsen

An upholstery application of "Pegasus." This man-made fiber is the result of a textile design collaboration of Amoco Fabric and Fibers Co. R & D department and Larsen Design Studio.

TEXTILE
"Etude"
DESIGN FIRM
Jack Lenor Larsen

"Etude," inspired by a Balinese motif,
is part of Jack Lenor Larsen's "Silk
Roads" collection.

TEXTILE
"Celestial, Lhasa Bouquet"
DESIGN FIRM
Jack Lenor Larsen

Printed on the iridescent silk satin of
"Celestial" are the ancient Tibetan
flower forms of "Lhasa Bouquet."

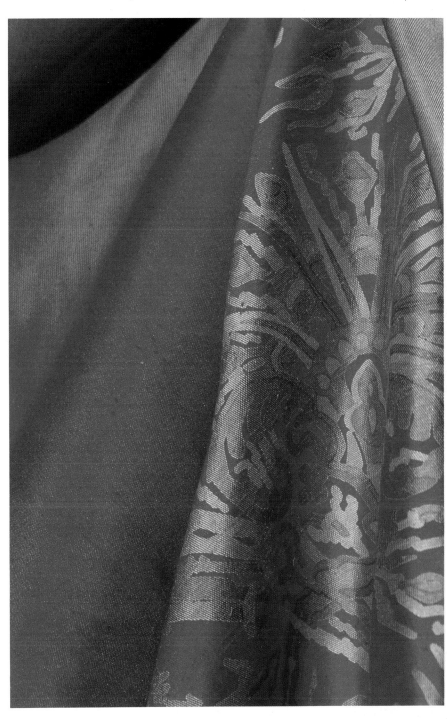

TEXTILE
"Misha"
DESIGN FIRM
Jack Lenor Larsen

Reminiscent of 17th-century Russian
embroideries, "Misha" combines the
versatility of a plain weave with the
elegance of a filigree pattern.

TEXTILE
"Pegasus"
DESIGN FIRM
Jack Lenor Larsen

"Pegasus" is woven of a man-made
textile created to mock the practically
indestructible properties of textiles
woven of horse hair. It is depicted
here applied to wallcovering panels
and upholstery.

TEXTILE
"Ombre Stripe"
DESIGN FIRM
Jack Lenor Larsen

A textile design from the "Silk Roads
Collection," "Ombre Stripe" has a
twilled weave structure derived from
ancient Thai silks.

TEXTILE
"Cybele"
DESIGN FIRM
Jack Lenor Larsen

"Cybele" is one of Larsen's "Galaxy"
collection of man-made textiles. This
iridescent fabric, available in ten colorways, is suitable for upholstery,
wallcovering and drapery
applications.

TEXTILE
"Nirvana, Celestial"
DESIGN FIRM
Jack Lenor Larsen

"Silk Roads" includes "Nirvana" (right).
The silk satin structure creates a bold
warp stripe on one face and reticent
shadow banding on the reverse.
"Celestial" is an iridescent silk satin.

TEXTILE
"Marble Art"
DESIGN FIRM
Jack Lenor Larsen

Inspired by the art of "commesse"
(decoration in marble and semi-
precious stone intarsia) popular during
the Italian Renaissance, is
"Marble Art."

Patti Lynn

New York, New York

Patti Lynn is a fashion designer and stylist in New York City. Her newest collection is of one-of-a-kind whimsical skirts and handbags.

She has worked for Vogue/Butterick and Nigel French, a trend forecasting company in London. She has done consulting work for many major manufacturers and retailers as well as international textile mills such as Iwanaka Woolens and Asahi Chemical (Japan), Santista (Brazil), John Kaldor (Australia), Anglo Woolens, Burlington and Milliken (U.S.A.).

TEXTILE/PRODUCT
"Pattibags and Pattiskirt"
DESIGNER
Patti Lynn
DESIGN FIRM
Patti Lynn

"Pattiskirt and Pattibags" show a full range of design possibilities using the Lamontage™ process.

TEXTILE/PRODUCT
"Plaid Art Pattiskirt"
DESIGNER
Patti Lynn
DESIGN FIRM
Patti Lynn

Because Lamontage™ fabric has structure the circle skirt shape is a natural choice. The "Plaid Art Skirt" introduces other materials like multi-twist yarn and ribbons into the unified structure of the fabric.

TEXTILE/PRODUCT
"Pattibags"
DESIGNER
Patti Lynn
DESIGN FIRM
Patti Lynn

A collection of Pattibags on a background of Lamontage™ fabric by Patti
Lynn. The designs take on a painterly
brushstroke quality using fuzzy fibers
or a more graphic quality using cut-
out motifs.

TEXTILE/PRODUCT
"Primitive and Optic Pattibags"
DESIGNER
Patti Lynn
DESIGN FIRM
Patti Lynn

An application of Lamontage™ fabric
on Pattibags. The pattern for Pattibags
is a single piece unit which snaps
together to form the functional
handbag.

TEXTILE
"Doggie Style"
DESIGNER
Patti Lynn
DESIGN FIRM
Patti Lynn

Inspired by **101 Dalmations**, is "Doggie Style" created in Lamontage,™ a process which layers many colors of fibers into unlimited designs. Lamontage is finished by needle punching all layers together into a soft fabric not unlike felt.

TEXTILE
"Stained Character"
DESIGNER
Patti Lynn
DESIGN FIRM
Patti Lynn

"Stained Character" was inspired by stained glass windows. Lamontage™ is neither printed nor yarn dyed. A 3-D effect is created by layering design motifs yet the fabric is unified by the needle punched finishing.

Quentel Mathis

Brooklyn, New York

Quentel Mathis, originally from Chicago, moved to NYC to be a writer. His creative talent led him to dancing. Then, as a statement of his political views and his desire to have a unique look, he painted his first pair of jeans for his own use. His uninhibited style attracted attention on NYC streets, which led to orders from private clients, and to a number of freelance assignments, including painted store window displays and hand-painted ties. His work can be seen at Patricia Fields, NYC. He continues to pursue his individual style in textile design and related endeavors.

TEXTILE/PRODUCT
"Primitive Tie-Dyed Gap Jeans"
DESIGNER
Quentel Mathis
PHOTOGRAPHER
Bill McConnell

"Primitive Tie-Dyed Gap Jeans" combine markings of sun yellow, turquoise, crimson, black, pink, brick, and dark blue in Quentel Mathis' unique style.

TEXTILE/PRODUCT
"Green Balls on Dark Blue Denim"
DESIGNER
Quentel Mathis
PHOTOGRAPHER
Bill McConnell

The bold patterns hand-painted on these denim jeans are done with flourescent paint which comes to life under black light.

TEXTILE/PRODUCT
"Silence = Death Faded Denim Jeans"
DESIGNER
Quentel Mathis
PHOTOGRAPHER
Bill McConnell

Quentel Mathis used a fork, ruler, and stencils to create the hand-painted patterns on "Silence = Death Faded Denim Jeans."

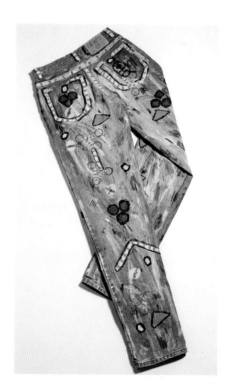

108

TEXTILE/PRODUCT
"Faded Denim Jeans with
Artists Signature Symbol"
DESIGNER
Quentel Mathis
PHOTOGRAPHER
Bill McConnell

The repeated "stick figure" symbol is
Quentel Mathis' signature symbol. It is
combined with a flowing stripe motif.

TEXTILE/PRODUCT
"Black Skirt"
DESIGNER
Quentel Mathis
PHOTOGRAPHER
Bill McConnell

"Black Skirt" combines a "Santa Fe"
stencil background with 'bleeding'
opaque white shapes outlined in
metallic blue, hand-painted in a 100
percent cotton.

TEXTILE/PRODUCT
"Red Crosses Shorts"
DESIGNER
Quentel Mathis
PHOTOGRAPHER
Bill McConnell

"Red Crosses" outlined with gold
metallic paint, surrounded by other
hand-painted brightly colored
markings represent "healthcare for
everyone - NOT warfare."

TEXTILE/PRODUCT
"Political Pants for the '90s"
DESIGNER
Quentel Mathis
PHOTOGRAPHER
Bill McConnell

These bleached faded denim jeans are
hand-painted with subtle political
symbols including Silence=Death,
Save the Earth, Pro-Choice, and Anti-
Apartheid symbols.

Sue McFall

Dunkirk, Indiana

Sue McFall creates colorful, evocative products using textiles upon which she applies a variety of techniques. The results are exciting garments and other constructions that activate the viewer's imagination. She is a full-time artist with studios in both Indiana and Florida.

TEXTILE
"Salad Dressing" (front view)
ARTIST
Sue McFall
MANUFACTURER
Sue McFall
USAGE
Wearable Art

"Salad Dressing" is a witty interpretation and play on words. It is lined, quilted, resist dyed and painted 12mm China silk.

TEXTILE
"3rd House of the Leopard"
"Housedress" series
ARTIST
Sue McFall
MANUFACTURER
Sue McFall
USAGE
Wearable Art

"3rd House of the Leopard,"
a ceremonial garment, is part of the
"Housedress" Series. It was created
with painted and resist dyed silk and
measures 52" w x 63" l.

Brooks Frank

Pallina

San Francisco, California

DESIGNERS
Cindy Alwan, Karen Schein
DESIGN FIRM
Pallina

Pallina is a fabric and accessories company that works in hand-painted, marbelized silk charmeuse fabric. Pallina is run by Cindy Alwan and Karen Schein, who design and manufacture all the Pallina products.

Pallina specializes in shawls, scarves, vests, hair accessories, and pillows of hand-marbelized silk, all with hand-rolled edges.

"Everything we do is geared toward having beautiful, luxurious products."

TEXTILE/PRODUCT
"Pillows"
DESIGNERS
Cindy Alwan, Karen Schein
DESIGN FIRM
Pallina
PHOTOGRAPHER
Benjamin Ailes

Pillows are one of the products Pallina applies their hand marbelized silk charmeuse textiles to, with beautiful results.

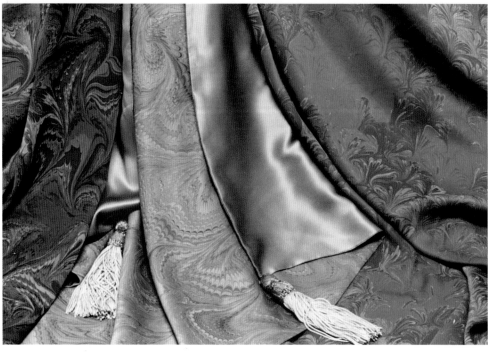

TEXTILE/PRODUCT
"Details"
DESIGNERS
Cindy Alwan, Karen Schein
DESIGN FIRM
Pallina
PHOTOGRAPHER
Benjamin Ailes

To achieve the marble finish, Cindy Alwan and Karen Schein mix their own acrylic colors, which are then floated on a water and gel solution a drop at a time. The colors are distributed in classic Venetian patterns using wooden implements. Four-foot-square pieces of silk are then carefully placed on the solution and allowed to absorb the color before being gently lifted off, rinsed, and hung to dry.

Dominique Ragueneau

Los Angeles, California

Dominique Ragueneau was born and grew up on the Mediterranean Rim, first in Tunisia where he was exposed to Arabic culture, then in the South of France.

He studied architecture in Marseilles. In the late '70s he entered the world of fashion in Paris where he worked with J.P. Brunet, Yves St. Laurent, and Bernard Chaix.

Dominique Ragueneau resided in New York City for most of the '80s where, inspired by the urban landscape, he created woven leather textiles in association with Calvin Mitchell, which were used in the design and manufacture of one-of-a-kind garments, jewelry, and accessories under the label "Doomey."

Since 1990, Dominique Ragueneau has lived on the Pacific Rim, in Los Angeles, continuing his work.

TEXTILE
"Woven Leather"
DESIGNER
Dominique Ragueneau
DESIGN FIRM
Doomey
PHOTOGRAPHER
Dominique Ragueneau

Dominique Ragueneau used metallic leather and metal rivets to create this exciting textile.

TEXTILE
"Woven Leather"
DESIGNER
Dominique Ragueneau
DESIGN FIRM
Doomey
PHOTOGRAPHER
Dominique Ragueneau

Four examples of leather woven through fishnet.

TEXTILE/PRODUCT
"Skirt in Woven Leather Through Fishnet"
DESIGNER
Dominique Ragueneau
DESIGN FIRM
Doomey
MODEL
Lori Eastside
PHOTOGRAPHER
Dominique Ragueneau

Leather is woven through selected areas of the fishnet in this piece, creating a variety of effects.

TEXTILE/PRODUCT
"Skirt in Woven Leather Through Fishnet"
DESIGNER
Dominique Ragueneau
DESIGN FIRM
Doomey
MODEL
Lori Eastside
PHOTOGRAPHY
Dominique Ragueneau

Leather is woven through selected areas of
the fishnet in this piece, creating a variety of
effects.

TEXTILE
"Leather with Pattern"
DESIGNER
Dominique Ragueneau
DESIGN FIRM
Doomey
CLIENT
Linda Lee
PHOTOGRAPHER
Dominique Ragueneau

Patterns of woven leather are inset
into larger pieces of leather. The insets
are attached with metal rivets.

TEXTILE/PRODUCT
"Jacket in Hand-painted Leather"
DESIGNER
Dominique Ragueneau
DESIGN FIRM
Doomey
MODEL
Lori Eastside
PHOTOGRAPHER
Dominique Ragueneau

A pastel-colored pattern hand-painted on leather was used to create this attractive jacket.

TEXTILE
"Painted Leather"
DESIGNER
Dominique Ragueneau
DESIGN FIRM
Doomey
PHOTOGRAPHER
Dominique Ragueneau

Examples of hand-painted leathers, some of which reflect Dominique Ragueneau's impressions of Los Angeles.

TEXTILE/PRODUCT
"Coat in Woven Leather"
DESIGNER
Dominique Ragueneau
DESIGN FIRM
Doomey
MODEL
Lori Eastside
PHOTOGRAPHER
Dominique Ragueneau

This "Coat in Woven Leather" is created without any sewing. It is constructed entirely with metal rivets.

TEXTILE/PRODUCT
"Jacket in Painted Leather"
DESIGNER
Dominique Ragueneau
DESIGN FIRM
Doomey
PHOTOGRAPHER
Dominique Ragueneau

A jacket created with hand-painted leather which includes a palm tree motif.

TEXTILE/PRODUCT
"Dress with Hand-painted Silk Chiffon"
DESIGNER
Dominique Ragueneau
DESIGN FIRM
Doomey
CLIENT
Harriet Selwyn
MODEL
Lori Eastside
PHOTOGRAPHER
Dominique Ragueneau

A delicate hand-painted pattern on silk
chiffon by Dominique Ragueneau applied to
a dress by Harriet Selwyn.

TEXTILE/PRODUCT
"Top in Heavy Woven Leather"
DESIGNER
Dominique Ragueneau
DESIGN FIRM
Doomey
MODEL
Lori Eastside
PHOTOGRAPHER
Dominique Ragueneau

A heavy woven leather textile, also used for
upholstery, made into an unusual top with a
fringed collar.

Christina Read

New York, New York

Born in Charlottesville, Virginia, in 1947, Christina Ham Read graduated from National Ballet School, in Washington, D.C. in 1965, and moved to New York City as a member of the Harkness Ballet. Forming her own contemporary dance company in 1974, she began to experiment with various media, and to paint.

She continues to exhibit her artwork in galleries and museums throughout the U.S.

TEXTILE/PRODUCT
"Napkin, Placemat, and Tablecloth #3"
DESIGNER
Christina Read
CLIENT/MFR
Artex Home Products
PHOTOGRAPHER
Andrew Garn

TEXTILE/PRODUCT
"Napkin, Placemat, and Tablecloth #4"
DESIGNER
Christina Read
CLIENT/MFR
Artex Home Products
PHOTOGRAPHER
Andrew Garn

Four place settings by Christina Read. Each a 22"
square napkin, 14" x 19" placemat, and 54"
tablecloth, all silk-screened cotton "momie" cloth.

TEXTILE/PRODUCT
"Placemats and Napkins"
DESIGNER
Christina Read
CLIENT/MFR
Artex Home Products
PHOTOGRAPHER
Andrew Garn

"Placemats and Napkins" are made
with silk-screened cotton "momie"
cloth. Placemats are 14" x 19", napkins
are 22" square.

Renata Rubim
Porto Alegre, Brazil

Renata Rubim was born in Rio de Janeiro, Brazil, in 1948. She studied weaving and graphic design in Brazil and surface design at the Rhode Island School of Design, with a Fulbright Scholarship. She has shown her work in 30 individual and group shows in Brazil, the U.S., Germany, and Belgium. Renata Rubim works for a variety of Brazilian companies as a textile and surface designer and as a color consultant. She has her own studio in Porto Alegre, in southern Brazil where she lives and teaches surface design at the local Museum of Fine Arts.

TEXTILE/PRODUCT
"Rug"
DESIGNER
Renata Rubim
MANUFACTURER
Companhia Dos Tapetes Ocidentais, Brazil
PHOTOGRAPHER
Leonid Streliaev, Brazil

Renata Rubim's "Rug" has bold patterns of earth tones, black, white and blue, that create an energetic rhythm.

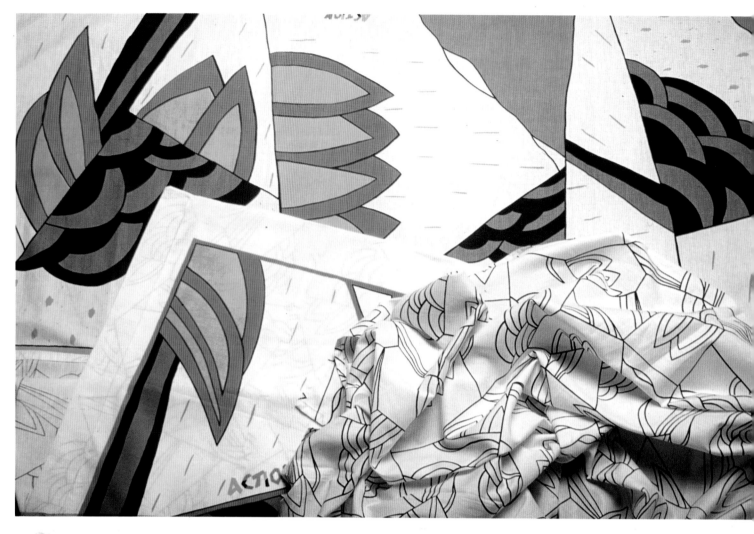

TEXTILE/PRODUCT
"Sheets and Pillow Case"
DESIGNER
Renata Rubim
CLIENT/MFR
Artex, S.A.
PHOTOGRAPHER
Leonid Streliaev, Brazil

Renata Rubim's design for "Sheets and
Pillow Case" is full of "action."

TEXTILE/PRODUCT
"Comforter and Pillow Case for Children"
DESIGNER
Renata Rubim
CLIENT
Tok & Stok, Brazil
PHOTOGRAPHER
Leonid Streliaev, Brazil

This textile design by Renata Rubim is
for application on children's comfort-
ers and pillow cases.

124

Scalamandré

Long Island City, New York

DESIGN FIRM
Scalamandré
REPRESENTED BY
The Manzone Group Ltd.

alamandré has produced quality tex-
es for over fifty years under the leader-
ip of three generations of the
alamandré family. Located in Long Is-
nd City, New York, the company's mill
oms thousands of pounds of silk, wool,
tton, linen and synthetic yarns produc-
g opulent carpets, damasks, liseres,
npasses, brocatelles, trimmings and wall
verings.

anco Scalamandré has received many
ards, including the American Historical
eservation Society medal, a gold medal
Americanism from the Colonial Dames
America, and the National Trust for
storic Preservation, among others.
ughter Adriana Bitter, President and
llow ASID, is an internationally re-
wned expert in textiles, whose knowl-
ge has been called upon by museums
d encyclopedias, and whose designs
orn Monticello, San Simeon, the World
nancial Center and countless other
orldwide projects.

TEXTILE
"Classical Lampas"
DESIGN FIRM
Scalamandré
USAGE
Multiple

"Classical Lampas" consists of
spun rayon, linen and silk.
Scalamandré originally reproduced
this lampas from a document for the
Los Angeles Music Center. Today,
"Classical Lampas" is available in 4
colorways. This lampas is being recre-
ated from a late 18th century lampas.

TEXTILE
"Cerises"
DESIGN FIRM
Scalamandré
USAGE
Multiple

"Cerises" is Scalamandré's attempt to
bring tapestry into the twentieth
century. The pattern is a rich display of
fruits and greenery, deep in tone,
which are presented in a tightly-
woven composition. This textile is
woven in France and is composed of
100 percent cotton.

TEXTILE
"Versailles 26042"
DESIGN FIRM
Scalamandré
USAGE
Multiple

"Versailles" is a woven lampas whose
pattern displays the highly fashionable
items of the eighteenth century:
ribbons, tassels, and plumes. It is
woven of 100 percent spun rayon.

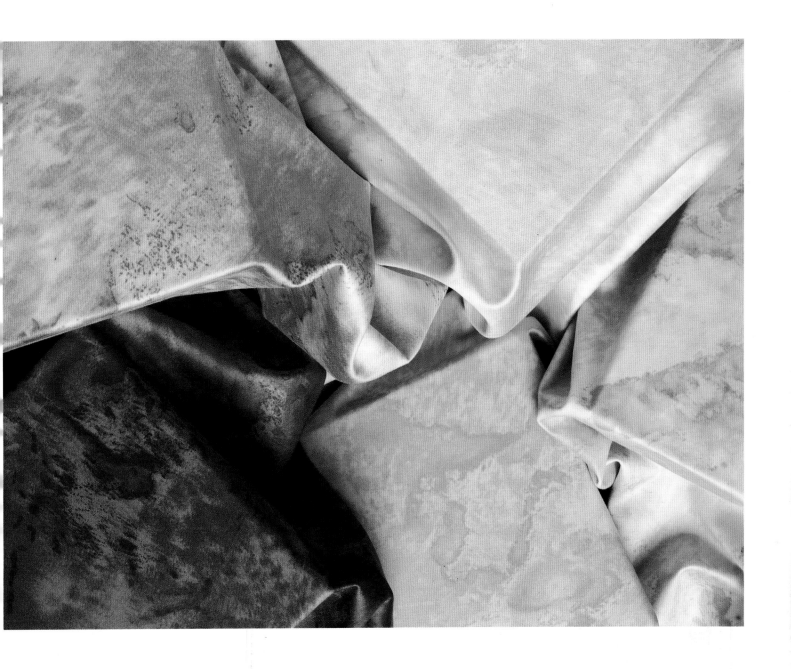

TEXTILE
"Georgian"
DESIGN FIRM
Scalamandré
USAGE
Multiple

"Georgian" is made of 100 percent
silk. The fabric is 50" wide, has a 24½"
vertical repeat and a 25" horizontal
repeat. Incorporated into its stark black
background is a historical floral
pattern.

TEXTILE
"Serigraph Stripe"
DESIGN FIRM
Schumacher
PHOTOGRAPHER
Susan Wides

"Serigraph Stripe" is printed over a
geometric jacquard pattern. It is
woven of 100 percent mercerized
cotton.

TEXTILE
"Tulip Tapestry," "Prairie Fern," "Imperial Crystals"
DESIGN FIRM
Schumacher
PHOTOGRAPHER
Susan Wides

"Tulip Tapestry" (bottom), and "Prairie Fern" (left) are derived from designs by Frank Lloyd Wright for the Avery Coonley House, built in 1906 in Riverside, Illinois. "Imperial Crystals" (right) is a reproduction of a fabric Wright designed for the Imperial Hotel in Tokyo. "Imperial Crystals" is woven of 50 percent wool and 50 percent cotton.

TEXTILE
"March Balloons," "Liberty Weave," "Imperial Squares"
DESIGN FIRM
Schumacher
PHOTOGRAPHER
Susan Wides

"March Balloons" and "Liberty Weave" are both derived from one of twelve graphic designs that Frank Lloyd Wright created in 1926. 'March Balloons' (top right) is a jacquard woven of 78 percent rayon, 12 percent cotton and 10 percent polyester. "Liberty Weave" (left) is woven of 100 percent spun rayon. "Imperial Squares" is one of the textiles that Wright originally designed for the Imperial Hotel in Tokyo. It is woven of 38 percent wool, 36 percent cotton, 18 percent acrylic, and 8 percent rayon.

TEXTILE
"Imperial Triangles II," "Imperial Squares"
DESIGN FIRM
Schumacher
PHOTOGRAPHER
Susan Wides

"Imperial Triangles II" is woven of 60
percent cotton and 40 percent rayon.
"Imperial Squares" is woven of 38 percent wool, 36 percent cotton, 18
percent acrylic, and 8 percent rayon.
Both are reproductions of textiles that
Frank Lloyd Wright designed and had
produced for the Imperial Hotel in
Tokyo, Japan.

TEXTILE
"Prairie Fern," "Prairie Mirage"
DESIGN FIRM
Schumacher
PHOTOGRAPHER
Susan Wides

These three textiles are derived from
designs by Frank Lloyd Wright for the
Avery Coonley house in Riverside, Illinois, 1906. "Prairie Fern" (top right) is
100 percent wool damask. A carpet
design for the Coonley house sup-
plied the idea for both "Prairie
Mirage" (right) and "Coonley Weave"
(left). Both fabrics are woven of 100
percent cotton and are 54" wide.

Frederic Schwartz

New York, New York

Frederic Schwartz is a partner in the firm Anderson/Schwartz Architects. He was a recipient of the Rome Prize in Architecture and a NEA Design Fellowship. He has been director of the New York office of Venturi, Rauch, and Scott Brown and worked for Skidmore, Owings, and Merrill. He graduated Phi Beta Kappa from the University of California at Berkley and received a Master's in Architecture from Harvard University in 1978.

Frederic Schwartz has been a professor at Columbia, Harvard, Yale, and the Univeristy of Milan, among others, and he has lectured extensively in America and Europe.

His work has been shown in numerous exhibitions, including the Venice Biennale, and is represented in the collections of many museums and univerisities.

Mr. Schwartz is currently designing sheets and towels for Cannon Fieldcrest, plates and silver for Swid Powell, furniture, carpeting, T-shirts, stage sets for a dance company in New York, and illustrations for a national children's magazine.

TEXTILE/PRODUCT
"Mondrian in Chartreuse on Bed of Roses and a Flowing Dress"
DESIGNER
Frederic Schwartz
DESIGN FIRM
Anderson/Schwartz Architects
ASSISTED BY
Janice Kitchen
MANUFACTURER
Tisca, Lyon, France
USAGE
Rug

The design for this rug is based on the juxtaposition of multiple layers of independent patterns and a dialogue between abstraction and figurative representation.

TEXTILE/PRODUCT
"New York, New York Rug"
DESIGNER
Frederic Schwartz
DESIGN FIRM
Anderson/Schwartz Architects
MANUFACTURER
V'Soske
USAGE
Rug

A collage of vibrant color and abstracted form make up the "New York, New York Rug." Designed by Frederic Schwartz and manufactured by V'Soske, the "New York, New York Rug" depicts the island of Manhattan. It is made of 100 percent wool and silk and measures 4'8" x 8'6".

TEXTILE/PRODUCT
"Leaves"
DESIGNER
Frederic Schwartz
DESIGN FIRM
Anderson/Schwartz Architects
GRAPHIC DESIGN CONSULTANT
Monica Banks
ASSISTED BY
Susan Mitnick
USAGE
Carpeting
PHOTOGRAPHER
Steve Moore

"Leaves" was designed as part of an overall motif for the Parkside Restaurant in Piedmont Park, Atlanta. Frederic Schwartz designed the plates and menus as well as the carpeting shown here, using leaves of different varieties as a theme.

Nina Sobell

New York, New York

Nina Sobell earned an M.F.A. at Cornell Univeristy, and a B.F.A. at the Tyler School of Art, Temple University. She has exhibited internationally and received awards from the National Endowment for the Arts, the Arts Council of Great Britain, and the New York State Council for the Arts. Sobell taught Electronic Imagery in the Design Department at U.C.L.A. and is presently Artist in Residence at the Interactive Telecommunications Program, Tisch School of the Arts, NYU.

Nina Sobell is a freelance artist, textile designer, and product designer.

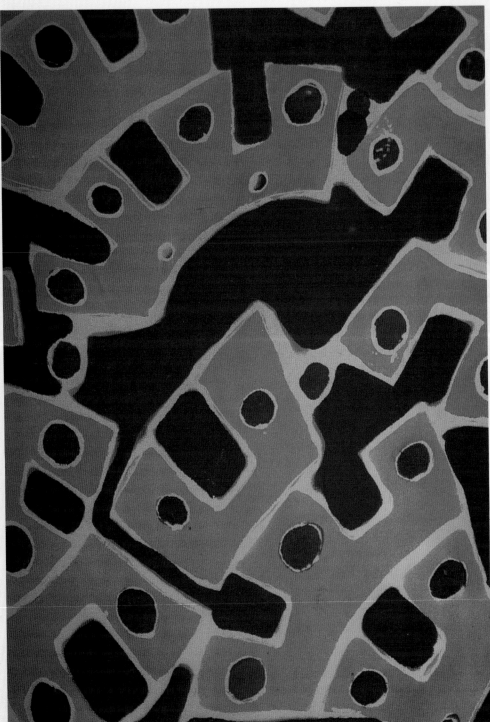

TEXTILE
"African Jewelry"
DESIGNER
Nina Sobell
DESIGN FIRM
Urban Castle
PHOTOGRAPHER
Peter Caminiti

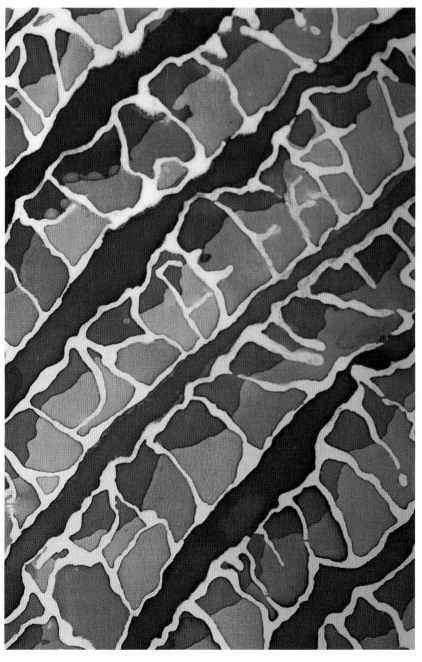

TEXTILE
"Spider"
DESIGNER
Nina Sobell
DESIGN FIRM
Urban Castle
PHOTOGRAPHER
Peter Caminiti

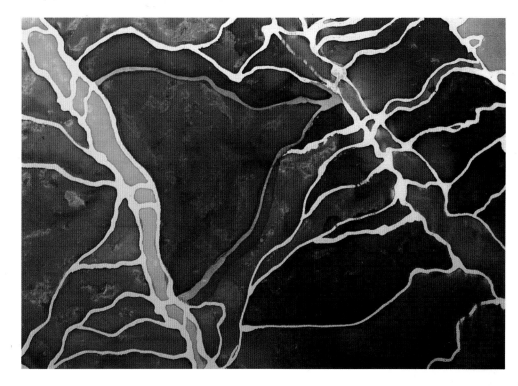

TEXTILE
"Grand Canyon"
DESIGNER
Nina Sobell
DESIGN FIRM
Urban Castle
PHOTOGRAPHER
Peter Caminiti

TEXTILE
"Lace Floral"
DESIGNER
Nina Sobell
DESIGN FIRM
Urban Castle
PHOTOGRAPHER
Peter Caminiti

TEXTILE
"Plum Leaves"
DESIGNER
Nina Sobell
DESIGN FIRM
Urban Castle
PHOTOGRAPHER
Peter Caminiti

Joel Sokolov

New York, New York

Joel Sokolov is a painter, drawer, printer, photographer, as well as furniture and textile/clothing designer/builder, and, now, author.

TEXTILE
"Floral-Textile #1"
ARTIST/DESIGNER
Joel Sokolov

TEXTILE/PRODUCT
"Floral Vest"
ARTIST/DESIGNER
Joel Sokolov

A vest made with the "Floral" fabric.

TEXTILE
"Vines"
ARTIST/DESIGNER
Joel Sokolov

A hand-painted textile titled "Vines."

TEXTILE
"Citi-Textile #1"
ARTIST/DESIGNER
Joel Sokolov

Two examples of unique, but related screen-printed cotton textiles in a city scape motif.

TEXTILE/PRODUCT
"Citi-Vest"
ARTIST/DESIGNER
Joel Sokolov

A lined vest made with "Citi-Textile."

TEXTILE
"Citi-Textile #2"
ARTIST/DESIGNER
Joel Sokolov

TEXTILE/PRODUCT
"Citi-Curtain"
ARTIST/DESIGNER
Joel Sokolov

A curtain made with the "Citi" design,
hand-screened on cotton.

Sofa Soma

New York, New York

DESIGNERS
Paula Zanger, Paul Fanfarillo
DESIGN FIRM
Sofa Soma

Sofa Soma is based in New York and specializes in hand-printed fabric for contract and residential commissions. Artist/Designers Paula Zanger and Paul Fanfarillo combine their talents to produce a line of eclectic fabrics with imagery ranging from classic sophistication to the avant-garde and eccentric. Ground materials include iridescent silk, cotton sateens, and vintage overprints.

Yardage and cushions are available at Barneys and Furniture of the 20th Century.

TEXTILE
"Assorted Iridescent Silks"
DESIGNERS
Paula Zanger and Paul Fanfarillo
DESIGN FIRM
Sofa Soma
PHOTOGRAPHER
Bill McConnell

An assortment of hand-printed motifs on iridescent silks.

TEXTILE
"Iron Curl Fabric"
DESIGN FIRM
Sofa Soma
CHAIR DESIGN
Peter Otsea

"Iron Curl Fabric" shown used as
upholstery fabric on a chair.

TEXTILE
"Column"
DESIGNERS
Paula Zanger and Paul Fanfarillo
DESIGN FIRM
Sofa Soma
PHOTOGRAPHER
Bill McConnell

Sofa Soma's "Column" textile is hand-
printed on cotton.

TEXTILE
"Spirit"
DESIGNERS
Paula Zanger and Paul Fanfarillo
DESIGN FIRM
Sofa Soma
PHOTOGRAPHER
Bill McConnell

The "Spirit" textile is hand-printed on cotton satine, shown here with a "Baroque" border.

TEXTILE
"Linea"
DESIGNERS
Paula Zanger and Paul Fanfarillo
DESIGN FIRM
Sofa Soma
PHOTOGRAPHER
Bill McConnell

"Linea" is hand-printed on woven acrylic awning stripe fabric.

TEXTILE/PRODUCT
"Bolster Pillow"
DESIGNERS
Paula Zanger and Paul Fanfarillo
DESIGN FIRM
Sofa Soma
PHOTOGRAPHER
Bill McConnell

A bolster pillow covered with Sofa
Soma's hand-printed "Linea" textile,
trimmed in Maribou.

TEXTILE/PRODUCTS
"Portfolio, Calendar, and Agenda Books"
DESIGNERS
Paula Zanger and Paul Fanfarillo
DESIGN FIRM
Sofa Soma
PHOTOGRAPHER
Bill McConnell

A portfolio, calendars and agenda
books constructed with Sofa Soma's
beautiful hand-printed textiles.

TEXTILE/PRODUCTS
"Ties"
DESIGNERS
Paula Zanger and Paul Fanfarillo
DESIGN FIRM
Sofa Soma
PHOTOGRAPHER
Bill McConnell

Vintage ties are overprinted with Sofa
Soma's unique textile designs.

Unika Vaev

New York, New York

DESIGNER
Suzanne Tick, Director of
Textile Development and Design
DESIGN FIRM
Unika Vaev, USA

Suzanne Tick worked for Boris Kroll Fabrics from 1981 through 1987 where, as vice president of design, she assisted in weaving and design development. From 1988 through 1990, she worked at Brickel Associates Inc. as director of textile design and development.

Ms. Tick received her B.F.A. from the University of Iowa with an emphasis on woven design. In addition, she earned an associate degree in applied arts at the Fashion Institute of Technology in New York City.

TEXTILE
"Pyramid"
USAGE
Home Furnishings
PHOTOGRAPHER
Luca Vignelli

"Pyramid's" pattern contrasts nicely against a marled yarn background. The marled yarn warp, achieved by twisting several colors, provides a look of subtlety and sophistication while being more interesting than a traditional heather. The color palette reflects a trend toward rich Renaissance colors combined with complex geological tones like gold, lapis, ruby and copper. Woven of 100 percent worsted wool, Pyramid passes the Wyzenbeek test for heavy duty use and the ASTM E-84 and California flammability tests.

TEXTILE
"Berries"
USAGE
Home Furnishings
PHOTOGRAPHER
Luca Vignelli

"Berries" is a traditional tapestry weave made on a jacquard loom with a technology that dates back to the mid-19th century. The scale of the rich leafy pattern is much smaller than 19th-century floral tapestries which makes this fabric appropriate for both traditional and contemporary designed seating. Each colorway highlights berries of a different hue with which a solid-colored fabric may be coordinated. This textile is woven more tightly than 19th-century tapestries, allowing it to pass heavy-duty wear abrasion tests and flammability tests.

TEXTILE
"Biedermeier Stripe"
USAGE
Home Furnishings
PHOTOGRAPHER
Luca Vignelli

This textile design is inspired by the design principles of classic Biedermeier furniture. The severity of the stripe itself is muted by minute squares whose subtle color transitions create a bridge through the fabric's palette.

The 14 colorways offer choices from an arresting black and white to the most refined tonal gradations. The Biedermeier Stripe can, therefore, be used in a surprising range of applications, from the easy curves of a Biedemeier chair to the most geometric contemporary designs. The high luster of the 100 percent worsted wool satin weave assures distinction of the fabric itself in any context.

TEXTILE
"Diamonds"
USAGE
Home Furnishings
PHOTOGRAPHER
Luca Vignelli

"Diamonds" is a traditional tapestry weave made on a jacquard loom with a technology that dates back to the mid-19th century. But its look is very contemporary, its geometric rectilinear architectural pattern gives "Diamonds" a modern look. "Diamonds" is woven more tightly than 19th-century tapestries, allowing it to pass heavy-duty wear abrasion and flammability tests.

"Diamonds" is available in five colorways. With six colors in the warp and two more in the weft, "Diamonds" highlights a myriad of solid color schemes.

TEXTILE
"Tahiti"
USAGE
Home Furnishings
PHOTOGRAPHER
Luca Vignelli

Originally used as a heavy coat fabric, for the military uniforms of the Danish Royal Guard, "Tahiti" is a "miltary twill" in the truest sense. While designed to complement Unika Vaev's newest brightly colored patterns, "Tahiti" also works well with most Unika Vaev patterns.
Made of 100 percent worsted wool of 19 ounces per yard, the fabric is heavier than other military twills and the clean, clear surface complements the brilliant hues achieved through piece dyeing.

Christine Van Der Hurd

New York, New York

Christine Van Der Hurd has produced designs in many different areas of the decorative arts. A sample of her varied commissions includes textile designs with Jack Lenor Larson, Donghia, and Kenzo, wall coverings with Osbourne and Little, scarves with Liberty of London, and bed coverings with J.P. Stevens and Wamsutta.

Christine Van Der Hurd has recently established herself as one of the foremost contemporary rug designers. She works both by commission in custom installations and on a limited edition basis. She has been commissioned to design rugs for the Henri Bendel store in New York for which she created ten different carpets. She also has created a number of limited-edition hand-tufted area rugs.

Christine Van Der Hurd is a graduate of England's Winchester School of Art.

TEXTILE/PRODUCT
"Water"
DESIGNER
Christine Van Der Hurd

"Water" depicts one of the four elements portrayed in the "Elements and Beyond" series. The 8' x 12' rug incorporates one of the designers favorite forms - the fish.

TEXTILE/PRODUCT
"Kaleidoscope"
DESIGNER
Christine Van Der Hurd
PHOTOGRAPHER
Rob Gray

"Kaleidoscope" is of 100 percent wool
yarns, hand-tufted. It is 8' in diameter
and part of the "… And So On"
collection.

TEXTILE/PRODUCT
"Moon and Stars"
DESIGNER
Christine Van Der Hurd
PHOTOGRAPHER
Rob Gray

Part of the "… And So On" collection,
"Moon and Stars" is a brightly-colored
6' x 9' hand-tufted rug made with 100
percent wool yarns.

TEXTILE/PRODUCT
"Air"
DESIGNER
Christine Van Der Hurd

"Air" is 9' x 9' of hand-tufted 100 percent wool yarns. Part of the "Elements Beyond" collection of carpets for the '90s, it depicts a large radiant sun surrounded by stars and bordered with crescent moons.

TEXTILE/PRODUCT
"Fire"
DESIGNER
Christine Van Der Hurd

"Fire" has a runner of royal purple edged in orange flames. It represents one of the four elements depicted in the "Elements and Beyond" series, and is 3'6" x 7'.

TEXTILE/PRODUCT
"Protozoa"
DESIGNER
Christine Van Der Hurd

This 5' x 7' rug "celebrates the minute cellular within nature." It is made with 100 percent hand-tufted wool yarns, and is one of the "Elements and Beyond" collection.

John Wolf

New York, New York

DESIGN FIRM
John Wolf Decorative Fabrics

The John Wolf Decorative Fabrics division of Cone Mills is a major decorative print converter in the United States who also services furniture manufacturers domestically as well as throughout the world. Through their parent company they own the Carlisle Finishing Company which is the largest printer of decorative fabrics in the United States.

TEXTILE
"Dawn"
USAGE
Home Furnishings

"Dawn," a contemporary floral, was created with designer's gouache in a 27" square repeat. Twelve colors were used to create this floral textile design.

TEXTILE
"Rebecca"
USAGE
Home Furnishings

"Rebecca" was develope●
to create a color wash te●
tonal effect was created v●

The Woven Image

Santa Fe, New Mexico

DESIGNER
Rebecca Bluestone
DESIGN FIRM
The Woven Image

Rebecca Bluestone is a fiber artist specializing in one-of-a-kind and limited-edition tapestries with a focus on the interplay of color and fiber. Each piece is handwoven in her Santa Fe, New Mexico, studio. She uses traditional tapestry and embroidery techniques with 100 percent hand-dyed wool.

"What I strive for in my work is a balance between formal structural design and my emotional response to color in all its subtle values, hues and intensities. By hand dyeing each color, I am able to study progressions of color and then working within these progressions, I attempt to find the emotion, the movement. The intent is to stimulate the senses, to move into the world of sensory perception, through the use of fiber, color, and design."

Rebecca Bluestone has exhibited her works in numerous galleries and museums in the southwestern United States.

Her education includes a B.A. from Oklahoma State University, as well as study with contemporary Hopi weavers.

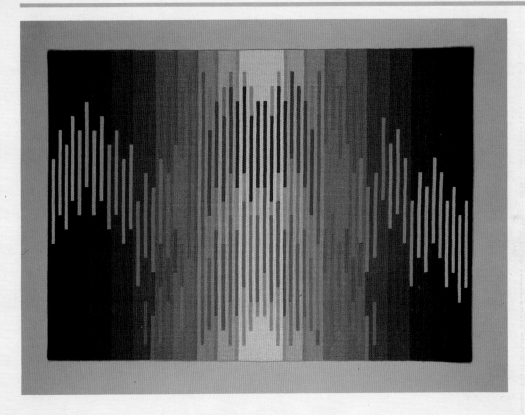

TEXTILE/PRODUCT
"Canonic Etude and Complement Study" series
ARTIST/DESIGNER
Rebecca Bluestone
PHOTOGRAPHER
Herb Lotz

"The 'Canonic Etude & Complement Study' series was inspired by the layers of sound in the music of the Baroque era."

PRODUCT
"Color Journey #1,2,3"
ARTIST/DESIGNER
Rebecca Bluestone
TEXTILE
100 percent hand-dyed wool
PHOTOGRAPHER
Herb Lotz

"The Color Journey" series is a
celebration of the sensuality of color;
an attempt to express the pure joy of
color, to stretch our ideas of what
color is and how it affects our lives,
our emotions, our ideas."

174

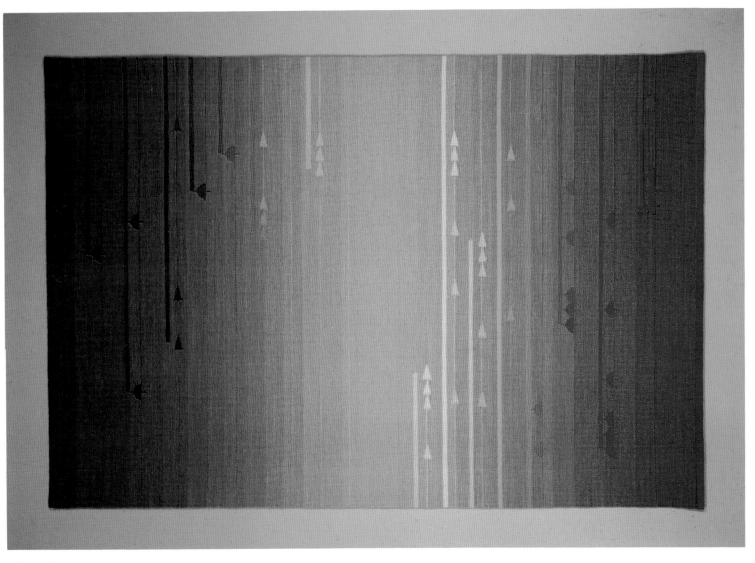

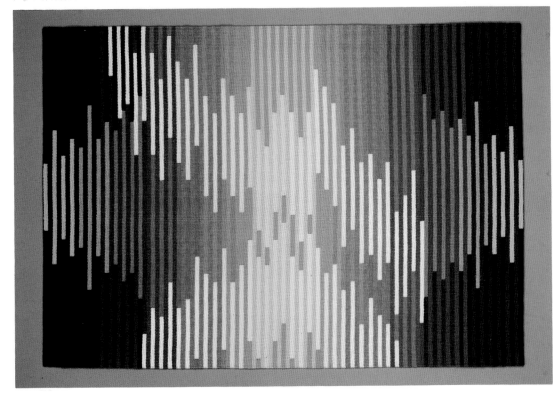

TEXTILE/PRODUCT
"New Music" series
ARTIST/DESIGNER
Rebecca Bluestone
PHOTOGRAPHER
Herb Lotz

"The 'New Music' series is inspired by the visual imagery of the music notation of the twentieth century. The interaction of color and fiber creates a sensory experience that moves beyond the scope of the notation's original intent."

Art Textiles

Michael Abrams

New York, New York

Michael Abrams considers himself "primarily a painter," who has been exploring the combination of painting and furniture. This process began with the creation of paintings on folding screens and has developed into the application of his painterly skills on a variety of home furnishings, many of which include hand-painted textiles.

He has had several solo exhibitions and has recently been a featured artist at Tiffany & Co., New York; Seibu Department Store, Tokyo; and Metropolitan Home's Showhouse II, a DIFFA project.

Michael Abrams received a B.F.A. in studio art and art history at Elmira College, Elmira, NY.

PRODUCT
"Scallop Chair"
ARTIST/DESIGNER
Michael Abrams
PHOTOGRAPHER
Jennifer Sloan

The "Scallop Chair" combines a scallop-shaped, hand-painted back, with unique legs and a patterned, textile-covered seat.

PRODUCT
"Dog Day Bed"
ARTIST/DESIGNER
Michael Abrams
PHOTOGRAPHER
Jennifer Sloan

"Dog Day Bed," made of
polychromed and leafed wood, has
textile-covered cushions and pillows,
all supported on a sculptural structure
with a dog motif.

PRODUCT
"Star Lounge"
ARTIST/DESIGNER
Michael Abrams
PHOTOGRAPHER
Jennifer Sloan

"Star Lounge" has a tufted cushion on
a painted and leafed cut-out structure.

Teresa Barkley
Astoria, New York

Teresa Barkley is a New York-based fiber artist who designs and creates distinctive wall quilts of the highest quality craftsmanship, drawing on 15 years of quilting experience. Many of her works bear a resemblance to a postage stamp design and are composed of a combination of historic textiles, commercially printed fabrics, heat-transferred images, and acrylic paint. Barkley's award-winning quilts have been exhibited internationally and are represented in corporate, university, and private collections. She lives in Astoria with her husband, Donald McLaughlin, and son, Ian.

TEXTILE/PRODUCT
"The Circus Stamp"
DESIGNER
Teresa Barkley
PHOTOGRAPHER
Bakal-Schwartzberg Studio, NYC

"The Circus Stamp" quilt is 58" x 68". Heat-transferred images of the 1966 postage stamp issued to honor the American circus appear on either side of the word "circus" which is painted on the banner over the tent.

TEXTILE/PRODUCT
"The Dawn of Television"
DESIGNER
Teresa Barkley
PHOTOGRAPHER
Bakal-Schwartzberg Studio, NYC

Sewn into "The Dawn of Television"
are the salvageable linen pages from a
turn-of-the-century Mother Goose
book, and pictures of TV cartoon
characters. Note the metallic TV
antennas between the rays of the sun
in this 45" x 54" quilt.

TEXTILE/PRODUCT
"Five Red Crosses"
DESIGNER
Teresa Barkley
PHOTOGRAPHER
Bakal-Schwartzberg Studio, NYC

"Five Red Crosses," a 22" x 22" quilt,
includes heat-transferred images of
five stamps issued to honor the Red
Cross.

TEXTILE/PRODUCT
"Great River Road"
DESIGNER
Teresa Barkley
PHOTOGRAPHER
Bakal-Schwartzberg Studio, NYC

"Great River Road" is composed of
four oval panels measuring 16" x 20"
and one round panel 10" in diameter.
"The concentric circles formed by the
quilting on these panels represent the
role our rivers play in connecting the
distant corners of our country." This
quilt consists of machine-pieced,
machine-quilted, machine-reverse-
appliquéd heat-transferred images,
(stamp and maps), and hand-painted
lettering.

TEXTILE/PRODUCT
"Vietnam Veterans Memorial"
DESIGNER
Teresa Barkley
PHOTOGRAPHER
Bakal-Schwartzberg Studio, NYC

This quilt was inspired by the strong
graphic design of the Vietnam
Veterans Memorial. The oval work is
made with machine-pieced, hand
reverse-appliquéd hand-quilted fabrics
and measures 20" x 16".

TEXTILE/PRODUCT
"Peacock Plaid"
DESIGNER
Teresa Barkley
PHOTOGRAPHER
Bakal-Schwartzberg Studio, NYC

"Peacock Plaid" was commissioned by the University of Delaware's College of Human Resources. The quilt is 69" x 53", machine-pieced, hand-appliquéd, hand-quilted, features hand-painted lettering and includes a heat transfer of a photograph. The imagery represents the artist's interpretation of the four steps of her own education: family, native, formal education and job experience.

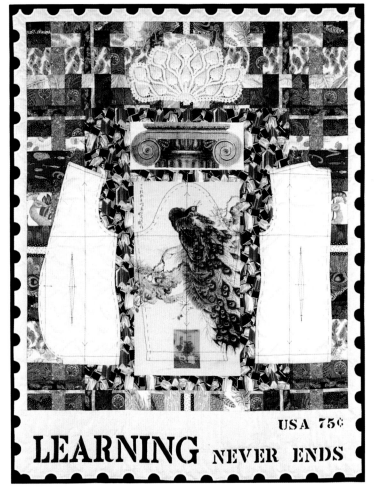

TEXTILE/PRODUCT
"How to Get a Husband Stamp"
DESIGNER
Teresa Barkley
PHOTOGRAPHER
Bakal-Schwartzberg Studio, NYC

This 50" x 53" quilt represents a totally fictitious stamp issued to honor the subject, "How to Get a Husband." Several suggestions on how to do just that are offered on the vintage handkerchief in the top left corner.

TEXTILE/PRODUCT
"Pacific Tears"
DESIGNER
Teresa Barkley
PHOTOGRAPHER
Bakal-Schwartzberg Studio, NYC

"Pacific Tears" is a depiction of the Exxon Valdez oil spill. The Pacific Ocean is depicted by salt sacks, Alaska by a map on a vintage tablecloth. The oil is pictured in droplets made of black leather. The work measures 83" x 101".

Chris Bobin

New York, New York

Chris Bobin's fabric assemblages are quilted appliqués, rich in color, texture, and humor. She has accomplished numerous commercial commissions for clients including Time, Inc., American Express/ Ogilvy & Mather, IBM, Gap International, and Sheraton, Inc. among others. Chris Bobin also has created custom props for notable productions including "Jerome Robbins' Broadway," "Saturday Night Live," and the Ringling Brothers and Barnum and Bailey Circus. Her work has been exhibited in numerous shows.

Chris Bobin received her B.F.A. at the School of Visual Arts, NY.

TEXTILE/PRODUCT
"Miss America"
ARTIST/DESIGNER
Chris Bobin
MANUFACTURER
Chris Bobin
PHOTOGRAPHER
Carl Picco

Another piece from the series "Careers for Women" is "Miss America." It is a 2½' x 3' fabric appliqué with objects.

TEXTILE/PRODUCT
"Chinese Girls"
ARTIST/DESIGNER
Chris Bobin
MANUFACTURER
Chris Bobin
PHOTOGRAPHER
Carl Picco

"Chinese Girls" is a fabric appliqué with found objects. It measures 4½' x 5' x 6' x 7'.

TEXTILE/PRODUCT
"American Food"
ARTIST/DESIGNER
Chris Bobin
MANUFACTURER
Chris Bobin
PHOTOGRAPHER
Carl Picco

Chris Bobin's 45½" x 63" piece, "American Food" is made with fabric appliqué and found objects such as crushed cans, cupcakes, carrots, cake, crackers and cheese, and a steak, all on a background of intoxicating beverages.

Ann Sherwin Bromberg

Brookline, Massachusetts

Ann Sherwin Bromberg came to weaving in the '60s, before which time she considered herself a painter. She combines the two processes with an additional dimension by integrating the planned visual composition into the structure of the canvas. Bromberg applies watercolor to the warp as she weaves, working wet as needed, creating a variety of effects.

Her works are included in numerous private and public collections.

She received her M.A. at the University of Cincinati, Cincinati, Ohio, and her B.S. from Cornell University.

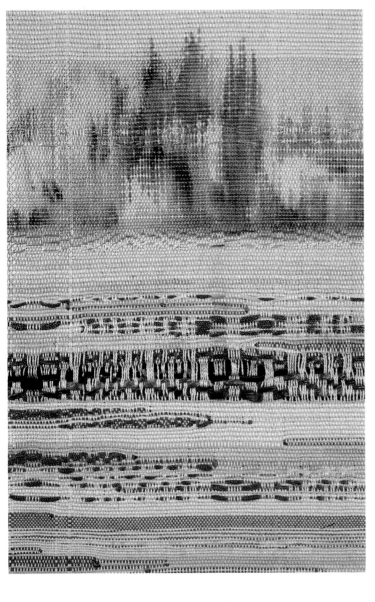

TEXTILE/PRODUCT
"Vision on Ice"
WEAVER
Ann Sherwin Bromberg

One can sense the cold and light of
the environment which inspired
"Vision on Ice."

TEXTILE/PRODUCT
"Back Bay in the Rain"
WEAVER
Ann Sherwin Bromberg

The combination of technique and
imagery creates an exciting interpretation of the Boston cityscape.

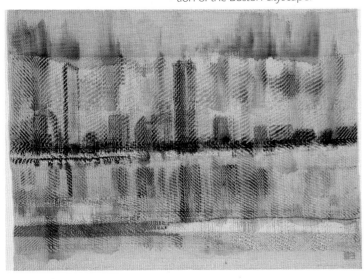

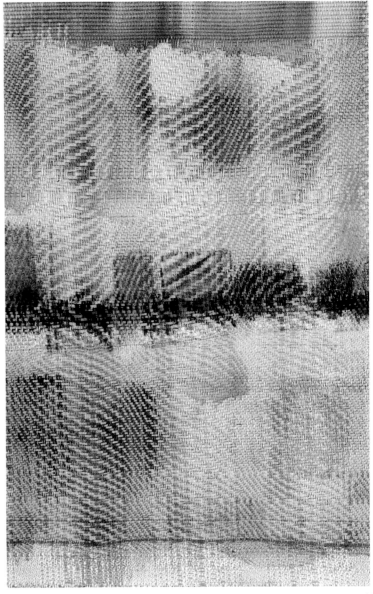

TEXTILE/PRODUCT
"From Malibu to Santa Monica"
WEAVER
Ann Sherwin Bromberg

This large-scale triptych wall hanging uses high-keyed color and exotic shapes to suggest the view "From Malibu to Santa Monica."

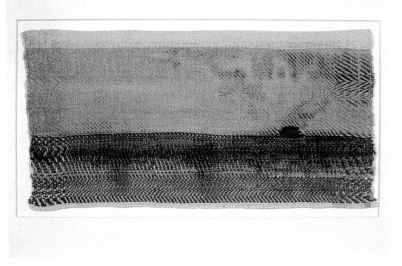

TEXTILE/PRODUCT
   "Santa Fe #1"
   "Santa Fe #2"
   "Santa Fe #3"
WEAVER
Ann Sherwin Bromberg

The light and pattern of Santa Fe is represented through the interplay of weaving and painting that is Ann Sherwin Bromberg's trademark.

Linda Leslie Brown

Boston, Massachusetts

Linda Leslie Brown comes from a fine arts background. Primarily a painter, she employs textiles in some works as collaged elements. In some pieces the imagery of the patterned fabrics becomes the subject matter. In others, textile motifs are integrated into painted motifs.

Linda Leslie Brown has exhibited her work in numerous New England venues and has received a variety of awards and honors for her artwork. She is presently an instructor at the New England School of Art and Design, and at the Rhode Island School of Design, where she teaches painting and drawing.

She received her Diploma from the Boston Museum School of Fine Arts and her M.A. from the Rhode Island School of Design.

TEXTILE/PRODUCT
"Night Park and Stars"
ARTIST
Linda Leslie Brown

"Night Park and Stars" was created with oil paint and collaged fabrics. The floral motifs of the collaged fabrics are interpreted and repeated with paint, creating the moody atmosphere depicted in the 18" h x 51½" w artwork.

Eugenia Butler
Los Angeles, California

Eugenia Butler, a Los Angeles-based fine artist, developed from a conceptual art background to product-oriented art activities. Along with her painting and drawing, she has created a large body of varied products, including chairs, tables and lamps. A whimsical dining-room suite by Eugenia Butler was featured prominently in the film "Ruthless People." Her designs for one-of-a-kind items and artworks, limited-edition chairs, and textile designs all have her signature energy and sense of motion. She is a graduate of U.C. Berkley.

TEXTILE DESIGN
"Nautilus"
ARTIST/DESIGNER
Eugenia Butler

"Nautilus" is a textile design based on the shell of the same name.

TEXTILE DESIGN
"Lucky Piece"
ARTIST/DESIGNER
Eugenia Butler

"Lucky Piece" is a textile design by
Eugenia Butler.

193

TEXTILE DESIGN
"7 League Boots"
ARTIST/DESIGNER
Eugenia Butler

The imagery combined in "7 League
Boots" evokes many varied interpretations.

TEXTILE DESIGN
"Lucky Piece"
ARTIST/DESIGNER
Eugenia Butler

"Lucky Piece" is a textile design by
Eugenia Butler.

Joyce Marquess Carey

Madison, Wisconsin

Joyce Marquess Carey's specialty is large scale site-specific, commissioned artworks for residential, corporate, and public spaces. Her work has been commissioned by several states including Florida, Alaska, Minnesota, and Wisconsin, as well as by many corporations, universities and private collections. Her work has been exhibited and published in numerous venues throughout the USA.

TEXTILE/PRODUCT
"Earl Grey's Garden"
ARTIST
Joyce Marquess Carey
CLIENT
Dean Medical Center, Madison, Wisconsin
PHOTOGRAPHER
Joyce Marquess Carey

"Earl Grey's Garden" seems to shimmer where it hangs at the Dean Medical Center in Madison, Wisconsin. It measures 13' x 21', and is composed of stitched pieces of fabric in a maze motif.

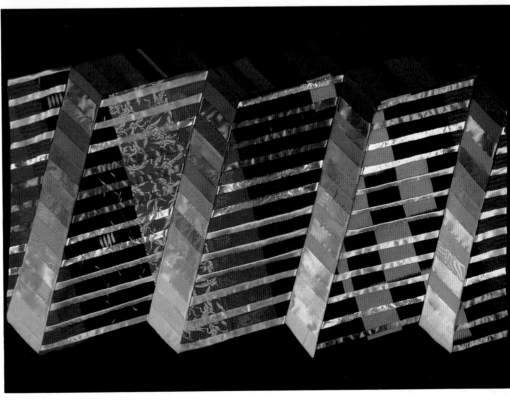

TEXTILE/PRODUCT
"Hako"
ARTIST
Joyce Marquess Carey
PHOTOGRAPHER
Joyce Marquess Carey

"Hako" is 24" x 40", a visual riddle
made with fragments of fabrics.

TEXTILE/PRODUCT
"Ribbon Candy"
ARTIST
Joyce Marquess Carey
CLIENT
Shriner Children's Hospital,
Minneapolis, Minnesota.
PHOTOGRAPHER
Peter Lee

"Ribbon Candy" is show installed at
the Shriner Children's Hospital in
Minneapolis. This cheerful work is 2.5'
x 10'.

TEXTILE/PRODUCT
"Building Blocks"
ARTIST
Joyce Marquess Carey
CLIENT
Univeristy of Mankato, Mankato, Minnesota
PHOTOGRAPHER
Joyce Marquess Carey

"Building Blocks" measures 5.5' x 19.5'
and is installed at the University of
Mankato, Mankato, Minnesota. It is a
beautiful example of Joyce Marquess
Carey's ability to make her flat wall
hangings seemingly jump from the
walls in three dimensions.

TEXTILE/PRODUCT
"Ribbon"
ARTIST
Joyce Marquess Carey
CLIENT
University of Alaska at Juneau
PHOTOGRAPHER
Dave Gelotte

Installed at the University of Alaska at Juneau, "Ribbon," by Joyce Marquess Carey, is 8' x 14'.

TEXTILE/PRODUCT
"Breaking Loose"
ARTIST
Joyce Marquess Carey
PHOTOGRAPHER
Joyce Marquess Carey

"Breaking Loose" is a visual riddle composed of fragments of varying types of fabrics. It is 45" x 65".

Margaret Cusack

Brooklyn, New York

Margaret Cusack has been stitching machine-appliquéd hangings since 1972. Included are "Skyscapes": large, architectural hangings that are abstract land and sky scape compositions. The surfaces are highly textural, dyed and padded to create rich imagery to enhance both corporate and residential environments. Other themes include stitched still lifes, portraits and American landscapes.

Margaret Cusack received a B.F.A. in Graphic Design from Pratt Institute, Brooklyn, NY.

TEXTILE/PRODUCT
"O, Christmas Tree"
ILLUSTRATOR/DESIGNER
Margaret Cusack

This colorful, appliquéd fabric sampler was created for use in a book of songs, published by Harcourt Brace Jovanovich, Inc. titled <u>The Christmas Carol Sampler</u>.

TEXTILE/PRODUCT
"Holiday Lane"
ILLUSTRATOR/DESIGNER
Margaret Cusack

Originally created for Macy's Department Store, this 22" x 28" fabric
collage has recently been licensed to
Different Looks and will appear as a
holiday euro tote bag.

TEXTILE/PRODUCT
"Shenandoah"
ILLUSTRATOR/DESIGNER
Margaret Cusack

This 20" x 30" fabric collage was
created exclusively as a poster used
extensively for the Broadway musical,
"Shenandoah." It appeared in subway
and newspaper ads, and was used as
the pictorial for the album jacket.

TEXTILE/PRODUCT
"Americana Quilt"
ILLUSTRATOR/DESIGNER
Margaret Cusack

This machine appliqué was created for
Good Housekeeping's, Good
Housekeeping - America's Favorite
Songs book.

TEXTILE/PRODUCT
"We Three Kings of Orient Are"
ILLUSTRATOR/DESIGNER
Margaret Cusack

Originally created for publication in a
song book The Christmas Carol
Sampler by Harcourt Brace
Jovanovich, Inc., this particular textile
was utilized in a Christmas card by
Unicef, United Nations Children's
Fund. Each textile is based on an
original illustration by the artist and
then constructed out of various fabric
scraps.

TEXTILE/PRODUCT
"George Washington Fabric Collage"
ILLUSTRATOR/DESIGNER
Margaret Cusack

This 25" x 33" collage was created for
an exhibition entitled "A Contemporary View of George Washington" at
the Fraunces Tavern Museum in New
York City.

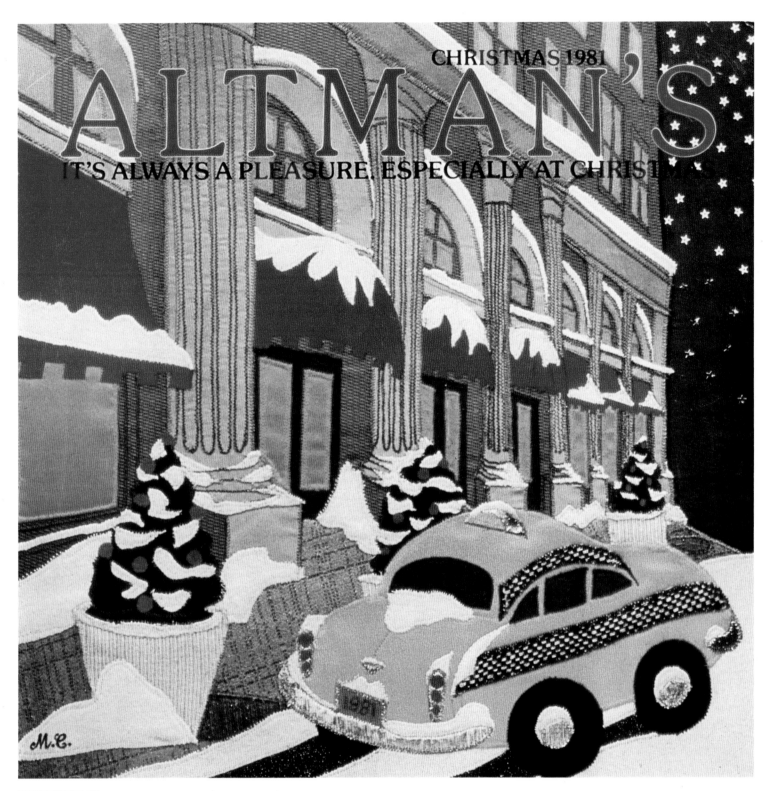

TEXTILE/PRODUCT
"B. Altman's Christmas 1981 Catalog Cover"
ILLUSTRATOR/DESIGNER
Margaret Cusack

This 19" x 19" collage was created in
three days for B. Altman's 1981
award-winning Christmas catalog
cover.

Mary Edna Fraser
Charleston, South Carolina

Mary Edna Fraser's batiks on silk are inspired by the "terraqueous" reaches of the continent - where earth, sky, and sea converge. This unique aerial perspective of our environment, "Islands from the Sky"© has, in 15 years' commissions, moved from flat images to sculptural drapes. Originally, photographs from her family's 1946 prop plane provided design inspiration. "Spacescapes," her newest body of work, is inspired by NASA satellite photographs.

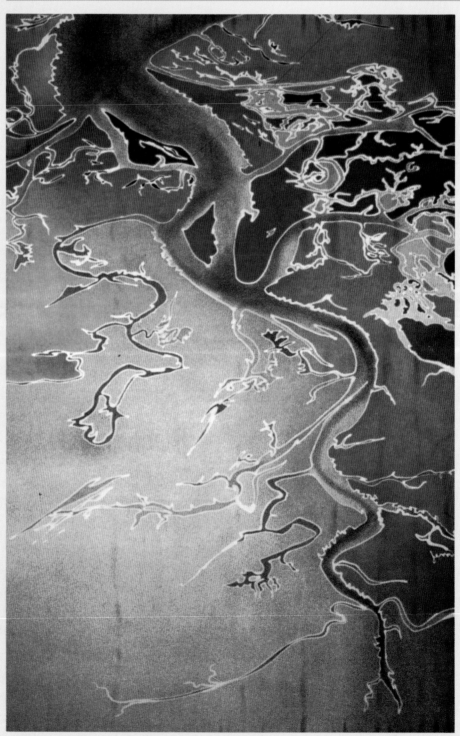

TEXTILE
"Broad Creek I"
DESIGNER
Mary Edna Fraser
PHOTOGRAPHER
Terry Richardson

"Broad Creek" is 76" x 46", batik on silk.

TEXTILE
"Misty Horizon"
DESIGNER
Mary Edna Fraser
PHOTOGRAPHER
Terry Richardson

"Misty Horizon" is another piece from the series, "Islands from the Sky." It is a diptych measuring 76" x 31", batik on silk.

TEXTILE
"Kiawah, SC"
DESIGNER
Mary Edna Fraser
PHOTOGRAPHER
Terry Richardson

Mary Edna Fraser's "Islands from the Sky" series includes this textile, "Kiawah, SC," a batik on silk measuring 108" x 72".

TEXTILE
"Charleston Coastline"
DESIGNER
Mary Edna Fraser
PHOTOGRAPHER
Terry Richardson

"Charleston Coastline" is a five panel batik on silk and measure 5'9" x 18'9". This topographically correct artwork is based on an aerial view of Charleston Harbor.

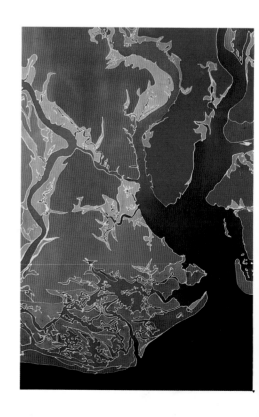

TEXTILE
"Ridges and Rivers"
DESIGNER
Mary Edna Fraser
PROJECT
Frederick W. Symmes Branch Library
CLIENT
Friends of the Library
ARCHITECT
Craig, Gaulden and Davis, Inc.
PHOTOGRAPHER
Terry Richardson

"Ridges and Rivers" is an aerial reflection of the mountain ridges, gorge and water surrounding the Symmes Library, where it is installed. Batik on silk panels depict a 5' x 12' view of the Appalachian Mountains.

TEXTILE/PRODUCT
"Charleston Waterways"
DESIGNER
Mary Edna Fraser
ARCHITECT
Richard Powell, LS3P
PROJECT
Charleston International Airport
CLIENT
Charleston County Aviation Authority
PHOTOGRAPHER
Terry Richardson

"Charleston Waterways" is a 74-yard sculpture of batik on silk, shown at its installation site, the Charleston International Airport. This sculptural design maps the coastline and penninsula of Charleston. Installed in May 1989, the piece was destroyed by Hurricane Hugo in September 1989. The work was recommissioned and re-executed.

Audrey Goldstein

Newton, Massachusetts

Audrey Goldstein designs textiles using figurative imagery as well as abstract repeat-patterned imagery. Her textile designs are an outgrowth of her background as a fine artist. She says, however, "I don't view applied design and fine arts as being essentially different."

Audrey Goldstein has exhibited her paintings, drawings, and paintings on stone in numerous group and one-person exhibitions. She has executed a variety of commissions for products made with her hand-painted textiles, most notably a series of large-scale curtains.

Ms. Goldstein has been a Massachusetts Artists Foundation Fellowship Finalist in both drawing and sculpture. She has taught at the New England School of Art and Design since 1979 where she is currently the chair of the Art Department.

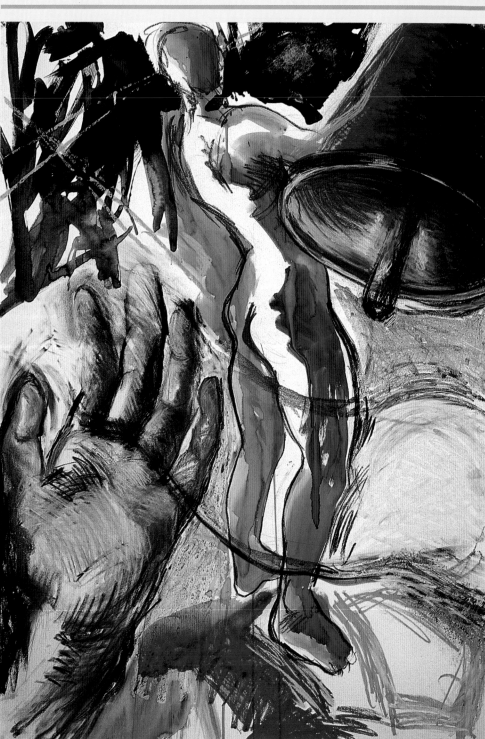

TEXTILE
"Piercing Ghanta"

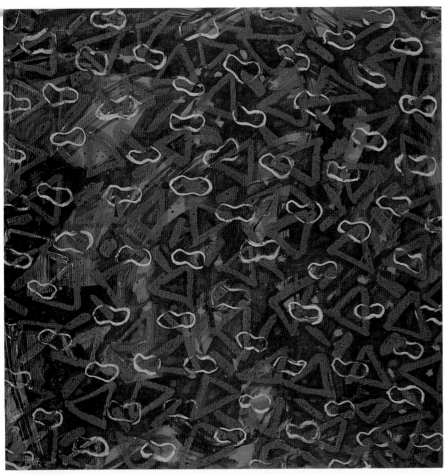

ARTIST/DESIGNER
Audrey Goldstein
USAGE
Multiple/Home Furnishings, Clothing
PHOTOGRAPHER
Mark Diamond

These textile designs employ basic shapes repeated to form patterns, each with a distinctive painterly touch. The color, line, and texture of the patterns create a playful, kinetic atmosphere suitable for a variety of uses.

TEXTILE
"Peanut Pattern"

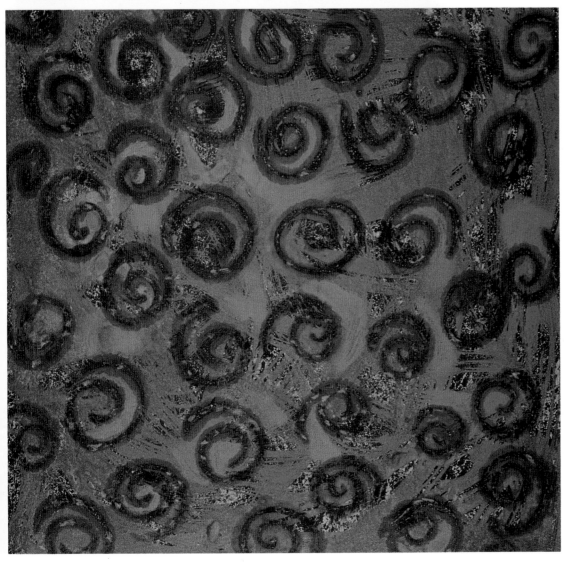

TEXTILE
"Cheerio Swirl"

TEXTILE
"The Princely Ones"
ARTIST/DESIGNER
Audrey Goldstein
USAGE
Curtain
PHOTOGRAPHER
Mark Diamond

"The Princely Ones" is an 8' x 12'
curtain, hand-painted on cotton. This
commission for an architect's residence is a stunning and innovative
use of textile design applied to
product design.

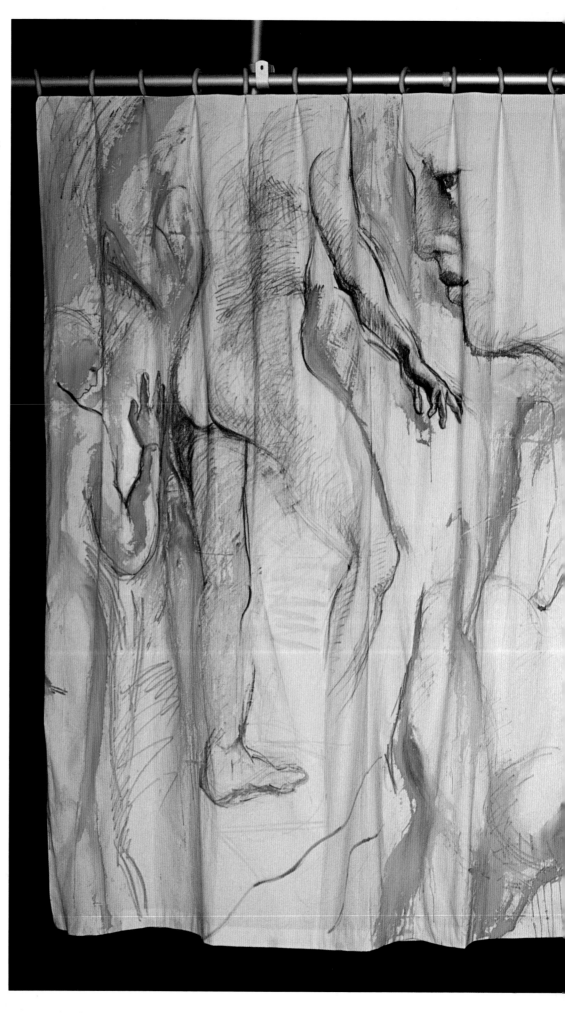

TEXTILE
"Etheral Flowers #2,5,6,7,9"
ARTIST/DESIGNER
Audrey Goldstein
USAGE
Multiple/Clothing, Home Furnishings
PHOTOGRAPHER
Mark Diamond

The "Etheral Flowers" series uses a traditional floral motif in a surprising variety of executions.

Terry Guzman

Teaneck, New Jersey

Terry Guzman works for a printing firm and works privately on her textile collages. She lives in New Jersey with her husband and their combined family of children.

Terry Guzman's textile designs have been widely exhibited. She received a B.F.A. from the Philadelphia College of Art.

TEXTILE
"Xmas Rose"
ARTIST
Terry Guzman

TEXTILE
"Ceiling Shadow"
ARTIST
Terry Guzman
COLLECTION
Ken & Alycia Wolfson

Terry Guzman's fabric collages are composed from a mosaic of fabric pieces adhered to stretched canvas. "Xmas Rose" is 12" × 16"; "Quiet" is 30" × 36"; and "Ceiling Shadow" is 44" × 44". The artist achieves a painterly effect with subtle changes of fabric, texture and color by using as a palette a variety of textile pieces.

TEXTILE
"Quiet"
ARTIST
Terry Guzman
COLLECTION
Marcia Wolfson

Janis Kanter
Chicago, Illinois

"Working with what is commonly referred to as a traditional medium, and developing it into a new and dynamic interpretation, is the emphasis of my tapestry weavings. I enjoy using a variety of fibrous materials, along with unexpected elements such as illuminated neon, to create textural effects and to heighten the visual impact."

"The underlying focus and meaning in my work places emphasis on the translations of an everyday human experience into a visual format. It is often the feeling of an enviromental energy or a universal testimonial in which a perosn might find themselves entangled."

"My art acts as friend, comrade-in-arms, analyst, sometimes enemy and, most often, mentor. It is the human adventure solidified through the eye."

TEXTILE
"Journey to Nowhere"
ARTIST
Janis Kanter
USAGE
Tapestry

This imaginative woven tapestry work is 3'w x 6' h. "Journey to Nowhere" has been exhibited throughout the West Coast in an exhibit called "The Divine Light."

TEXTILE
"Windy City"
ARTIST
Janis Kanter
USAGE
Tapestry

This 9'w x 8'h diptych tapestry with neon tubing was done as a commission for Windy City, Inc., in Vienna, Va.

TEXTILE
"From Plight Comes Light"
ARTIST
Janis Kanter
USAGE
Tapestry

"From Plight Comes Light," a tapestry weaving with neon tubing, is 7'w x 4'h. It is installed at the K.A.M. Group collection in NYC.

Janet Kuemmerlein
Prairie City, Kansas

Fiber artist Janet Kuemmerlein has achieved international stature for her outstanding work in textile design. Represented in the collections of the Museum of Contemporary Crafts in New York City and the Chicago Art Institute, Janet Kuemmerlein's textiles have been widely exhibited in museums and galleries throughout the United States and Europe. Her wide appeal is reflected in the extensive list of clients for her commissioned works, including Rochester Institute of Technology, numerous banks and corporations, churches, municipal buildings and hotels. A lecturer and juror for major art competitions, Ms. Kuemmerlein has also been a consultant and review panelist for the National Endowment for the Arts.

Born in Detroit, Michigan, Janet Kuemmerlein studied painting at the Center for Creative Studies and sculpture and metalsmithing at Cranbrook Academy, Bloomfield, MI.

PRODUCT
"Fiber Sculpture for Esson Residence"
ARTIST/DESIGNER
Janet Kuemmerlein

Dramatically placed above the fireplace in this contemporary residence, the fiber sculpture contains beautifully-hued earthtones twisted into a cyclonic shape.

PRODUCT
"Free Form Fish Bowl"
ARTIST/DESIGNER
Janet Kuemmerlein

A fabric bowl-shaped sculpture was
created using fiber and paint.

PRODUCT
"Arctic Echoes"
ARTIST/DESIGNER
Janet Kuemmerlein

This exuberant 5½' x 50' sculpture
hangs in the Anchorage, Alaska,
Library.

Therese May

San Jose, California

"I started out as a painter and then I switched to quiltmaking. For a while I alternated between the two. Now I paint on quilts. I like the element of risk involved with finishing a quilt that takes weeks or months to do and then painting on it with the possibility of ruining it. I am basically an expressionist and that is the way I sew, too. I start out with a drawing which I use for a pattern to cut my fabric pieces. These are pinned to a muslin backing and then I machine appliqué. I do not cut my threads, instead I let them form a network-like texture over the surface of the quilt. The images are fairly intuitive—fantasy plants and animals—fun stuff."

Therese May has degrees from the University of Wisconsin, Madison, and San Jose State Univeristy, San Jose, California. She has exhibited throughout the U.S., Europe, and Japan.

TEXTILE/PRODUCT
"Prosperity"
ARTIST
Therese May
PHOTOGRAPHER
Curtis Fukuda

"Prosperity," a 64" x 64" quilt, is made with acrylic paint on stitched fabric.

"Faith" (detail)

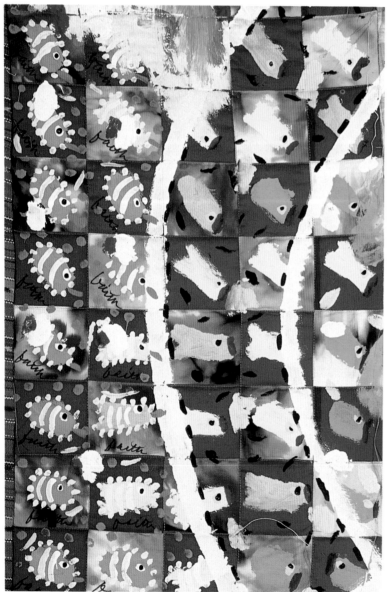

TEXTILE/PRODUCT
"Faith"
ARTIST
Therese May
PHOTOGRAPHER
Curtis Fukuda

"Faith," the title of which appears on the quilt itself, has a whimsical fish motif. It is 52" x 55", stitched fabric with acrylic paint.

Gudrun Mertes-Frady

New York, New York

Gudrun Mertes-Frady was born in Cologne, Germany, where she studied art at the Kolner Werschule. In 1981 she moved to New York. Her work has been exhibited in Europe and the United States.

TEXTILE
"Textile Designs"
ARTIST/DESIGNER
Gudrun Mertes-Frady
PHOTOGRAPHER
Peter Accatola

Pictured are designs for textiles by Gudrun Mertes-Frady.

Dottie Moore

Rock Hill, South Carolina

"The sewing machine is my tool. I use it as a painter uses the brush to convey visually intangible thoughts. My inspiration comes from the natural environment. My deep love and respect for the land developed while living in the Appalachian Mountains where the shapes and textures of the rolling landscape and the beauty of the wildflowers were invitations to rediscover the familiar. Textiles are symbolic to me of the importance of feminine power."

TEXTILE
"Windows"
ARTIST
Dottie Moore
PHOTOGRAPHER
Image Plus

"Windows" is 70" x 44", quilted textiles. It was inspired by the designer's rural environment and it includes one of Dottie Moore's repeated favorite subjects, trees, about which she says, "I love the variety of forms; I study the different directions of the limbs and wonder what influenced their growth.

"Appalachian Afternoon" (detail)

TEXTILE
"Appalachian Afternoon"
ARTIST
Dottie Moore
PHOTOGRAPHER
Jason Lee Moore

This quilt, "Appalachian Afternoon," is 62" x 70". The designer first does a sketch, makes templates, cuts fabric pieces, hand bastes, then works a satin stitch around the edges. She then adds border strips, batting and backing, and finally adds details with hand-embroidered stitches.

The NAMES Project
AIDS Memorial Quilt

Sponsored by the NAMES Project Foundation

San Francisco, California

Four years since its inception, the NAMES Project AIDS Memorial Quilt includes more than 15,000 individual 3' x 6' memorial panels. By organizing and displaying the Quilt, the goals of the NAMES Project are to:
- Illustrate the enormity of the AIDS epidemic by showing the humanity behind the statistics;
- Provide a positive and creative means of expression for those whose lives have been touched by the epidemic;
- Raise vital funds and encourage support for people living with HIV/AIDS and for their loved ones.

The NAMES Project Foundation has Chapters in 32 U.S. cities and 24 independent Quilt initiatives around the world.
Currently, the Quilt is the size of 5.6 football fields without a walkway in between each 12' x 12' section, or 8.75 football fields with a walkway between each 12' x 12' section. Over 26 countries have contributed panels to the Quilt. Some of the materials in the Quilt include: clothing, dolls, buttons, carpet, silk flowers, credit cards, wedding rings, human hair, fur, etc. The Quilt contains panels for many including: Rock Hudson, Liberace, Keith Haring, Ryan White, Perry Ellis, Roy Cohn, Robert Mapplethorpe.
To date, the Quilt represents 13.2 percent of all U.S. AIDS deaths and 2.8 percent of AIDS deaths worldwide. For more information, please contact the NAMES Project Foundation. See the appendix for the address.

PRODUCT
"The NAMES Project AIDS Memorial Quilt"
PHOTOGRAPHER
Richard Strauss

This outdoor aerial view of the Quilt was taken on Columbus Day weekend 1989, on the Ellipse in Washington, D.C. At that time there were 10,848 individual 3' x 6' panels. Today, the Quilt is comprised of more than 15,000 panels.

PRODUCT
"The NAMES Project AIDS Memorial Quilt"
PHOTOGRAPHER
Marc Geller

Three men create a panel for a loved one. The panel is now part of the Names Project AIDS Memorial Quilt.

Photos reprinted courtesy of the NAMES Project Foundation.

PRODUCT
"Panel for Michael Magni Johnson"
PHOTOGRAPHER
Marc Geller

This 3' x 6' memorial panel represents one of the 15,000 that currently comprise the Quilt today. Every day, more panels are added to the Quilt.

PRODUCT
"The NAMES Project AIDS Memorial Quilt"
PHOTOGRAPHER
Marc Geller

This photo shows how 8 individual panels are sewn together to create a 12' x 12' section.

Marilyn Price

Indianapolis, Indiana

Marilyn Price is an accomplished textile designer using silk-screen and quilting techniques to form her mostly large-scale products.

She has exhibited her works in a large number of juried, invitational, and one-artist exhibitions. Ms. Price's list of commissioned works for both private and public spaces is extensive.

Marilyn Price received her B.F.A. from Pittsburg State University, Pittsburg, KS, and her M.F.A. from the instituto de Allende, San Miguel de Allende, Guanajuato, Mexico.

TEXTILE
"One More Dance"
ARTIST/DESIGNER
Marilyn Price
PHOTOGRAPHER
Marilyn Price

A 4' x 5' piece, "One More Dance" was constructed of photo silk-screened and quilted cotton.

TEXTILE
"GTE Commission"
ARTIST/DESIGNER
Marilyn Price
CLIENT
GTE Corp., Fort Wayne, IN
PHOTOGRAPHER
Marilyn Price

This piece is 4' x 4½', photo silk-screened and quilted cotton.

TEXTILE
"Riley Hospital Commission"
ARTIST/DESIGNER
Marilyn Price
CLIENT
Indiana University Riley Hospital,
Indianapolis, IN
PHOTOGRAPHER
Marilyn Price

A 3½' x 10' work constructed of
screen-printed and quilted cotton
shown in the hospital where it is
installed.

TEXTILE
"Inner Rhythms, Outer Voices"
ARTIST/DESIGNER
Marilyn Price
DESIGN FIRM
Eden Designs, Indianapolis, IN
PHOTOGRAPHER
Marilyn Price

A 30″ textile detail. "Inner Rhythms, Outer Voices," is made of quilted linen utilizing photo-screened images. It is installed at Huntington College. Huntington, IN.

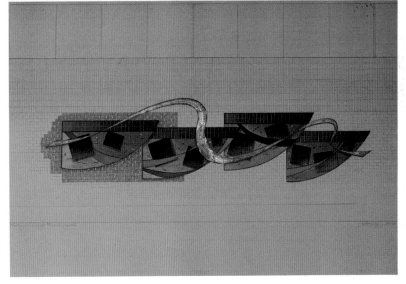

TEXTILE
"Morris Plan Commission"
CLIENT
Morris Plan Inc., Evansville, IN.
ARTIST/DESIGNER
Marilyn Price
INTERIOR DESIGNER
Chris Buck
AGENT
New Harmony Gallery of
Contemporary Art, New Harmony, IN.
PHOTOGRAPHER
Marilyn Price

This piece is 5' x 16', made of screen-printed and quilted linen.

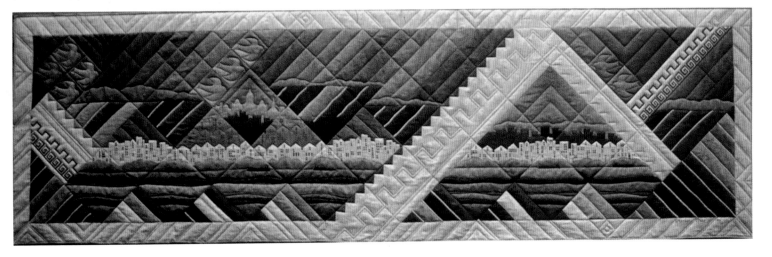

Peter and Paul Stasek

Mannheim, Germany

Peter and Paul Stasek have been engaged in artistic concepts for interior design, development of furniture objects, and sculptures in limited editions, as well as in the creation of numerous tapestry works.

Peter Stasek was born in Prague in 1955 and received his diploma at the NAB Weimar-Dept. of Architecture.

Paul Stasek was born in Prague in 1957 and earned his Diploma at the Technical Univeristy for Architecture in Prague.

TEXTILE/PRODUCT
"The Heaven of Jerusalem"
DESIGNERS
Peter and Paul Stasek
SITE
Synagogue, Mannheim, Germany
ARCHITECT
Karl Schmecker
PHOTOGRAPHER
Werbeverlag Gorzinski

"The Heaven of Jerusalem" shown here in a view through the chandelier, a tapestry cover of a synagogue dome, divided into 16 segments. A side effect of the use of a large tapestry on the ceiling is the improvement of the room's acoustics.

The techinique involved in Peter and Paul Stasek's tapestries could be called "fiber painting." Dyed wool fleeces are manually laid one over the other in thin layers on a backing of jute and are spread out in such a way that a flowing structure is created.

The dome depicted here is 10.70 m.

TEXTILE/PRODUCT
"Peeping Feathers"
DESIGNERS
Peter and Paul Stasek
PHOTOGRAPHER
Siegfried Herrmann

This tapestry, "Peeping Feathers," is 133 cm. x 180 cm. It is made with Peter and Paul Stasek's 'fiber painting' technique, for which a special machine is employed, using 10,000 needles to pull a portion of the fleece fibers into the backing material. For this tapestry manufacturing technique, the designers have registered the protected trademark ARTFIL ®.

TEXTILE/PRODUCT
"World of Destroyed Mirror"
DESIGNERS
Peter and Paul Stasek
PHOTOGRAPHER
Siegfried Herrmann

"World of Destroyed Mirror" is a tapestry, 138 cm. x 180 cm.

TEXTILE/PRODUCT
"Dactylopterus"
DESIGNERS
Peter and Paul Stasek
PHOTOGRAPHER
Werbeverlag Gorzinski

"Dactylopterus," by Peter and Paul Stasek, is a 500 cm. x 300 cm. room divider of wood and tapestry surfaces in linen, in the shape of a primitive flying fish.

TEXTILE/PRODUCT
"The Anthology of Water"
DESIGNERS
Peter and Paul Stasek
PHOTOGRAPHER
Siegfried Herrmann

"The Anthology of Water," a tapestry
ceiling, and lighting by Peter and Paul
Stasek, is installed at the wine-tasting
cellar of the Vollmer Winery in the
Roman tower in Ellerstadt,
(Wachenheim), Germany. The
diameter of the octagon ceiling is 6
meters.

TEXTILE/PRODUCT
"Scenario Ignoto"
DESIGNERS
Peter and Paul Stasek
SITE
Lutheran Church in Wachenheim,
Germany
PHOTOGRAPHER
Siegfried Herrmann

"Scenario Ignoto" is a tapestry installed
at the front of a Lutheran church in
Wasenheim, Germany. The dimensions of the work are 4.5 m. x 7.12 m.

Jill Wilcox

Brooklyn, New York

Jill Wilcox, primarily a painter, has worked as a textile designer for the past several years. She has a B.A. in Art from Sonoma State University and studied at the Pacific Basin School of Textile Arts, Berkeley; the San Francisco School of Fabric Art; and at F.I.T. in NYC.

"Dual interests have lead me to making large-scale painted (sometimes appliquéd) works on fabric, happily blurring the boundaries of painting and textile design."

TEXTILE/PRODUCT
"Trees #2"
ARTIST/DESIGNER
Jill Wilcox
USAGE
Tapestry
PHOTOGRAPHER
Dave King

This is another in the series of monotone, soft focus tree tapestries. It is 4' x 5', textile paint on cotton canvas.

TEXTILE/PRODUCT
"Division"
ARTIST/DESIGNER
Jill Wilcox
USAGE
Tapestry
PHOTOGRAPHER
Dave King

"Division," a tapestry measuring 3½' x
5½', was made with textile paint on
cotton canvas with painted canvas
appliqués. Note the innovative
hanging method of this piece.

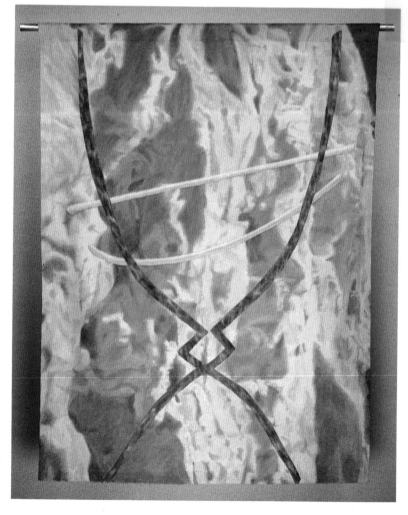

TEXTILE/PRODUCT
"Ice View"
ARTIST/DESIGNER
Jill Wilcox
USAGE
Tapestry
PHOTOGRAPHER
Dave King

"Ice View" is a view of a glacier face,
with a linear motif in the foreground.
This tapestry is 3½' x 5', painted on
cotton canvas with painted canvas
appliqués.

Windlines

Santa Monica, California

Banner artist Sylvia Gentile specializes in creating fabric installations that dramatically enhance architectural spaces. Innovative designs, appliquéd, hand-painted or woven on richly colored nylon, vinyl mesh, canvas, or silk are characteristic of Windlines' work.

Sylvia Gentile's art has been commissioned by Xerox, the City of Santa Monica, the City of Beverly Hills, and the California Crafts Museum, among many other corporate and private collections. She has won grants from the Santa Monica Arts Commission, and the Security Pacific Bank Foundation.

She earned a B.A. in East Asian Studies and Studio Art from Oberlin College.

TEXTILE/PRODUCT
"Third Street Promenade —
Santa Monica, California"
DESIGNER
Sylvia Gentile
CLIENT
Bayside District Corp., City of Santa Monica
PHOTOGRAPHER
Deborah Roundtree

The Third Street Promenade in Santa Monica is home for 18 appliquéd banners, five colors each, 6½' x 12' each. There are four different designs on the 3-block walk. The banners are made with cordura nylon, vinyl mesh, and gold lamé.

TEXTILE/PRODUCT
"Santa Monica Public Library
- Main Reading Room"
DESIGNER
Sylvia Gentile
CLIENT
Santa Monica Public Library
Executive Board
PHOTOGRAPHER
Scott Torrance

Sylvia Gentile's textile installation at the
Santa Monica, CA , Public Library
main reading room is made up of five
9' x 9' parabaloid shapes suspended
in a 44' x 88' space. It is made with
canvas with colored dyes and
styrofoam accent shapes.

TEXTILE/PRODUCT
"Colorado Place"
DESIGNER
Sylvia Gentile
CLIENT
Southmark Pacific Corporation
PHOTOGRAPHER
Deborah Roundtree

The twenty 4' x 12' appliquéd banners
in three different designs that are
installed at Colorado Place in Santa
Monica, California, are made with
nylon and vinyl mesh.

TEXTILE/PRODUCT
"Alhambra Design Center"
DESIGNER
Sylvia Gentile
CLIENT
Taehee Lee Architects and
Pinki Chen, Developer
PHOTOGRAPHER
Deborah Roundtree

Six 2¹/₂' x 12' appliquéd, layered,
rectangular banners and four 2' x 4'
appliquéd, layered banners make up
the installation at the Alhambra,
California, Design Center. They are
made with acrylic canvas.

Index

DESIGNERS

Appendix

Michael J. Abrams
664 6th Avenue
New York, NY 10010

Adam James Textiles, Inc.
59 Gilpin Avenue
Smithtown, NY 11787

Barbara Gras
Rua Laerte Assuncao 413
Jardin Paulistano, Sao Paulo
SP 01 444, Brazil

Teresa Barkley
24-40 27th Street
Astoria, NY 11102

Chris Bobin
c/o Fabric Effects
20 W. 20th Street/5th Floor
New York, NY 10011

Naomi Boccio
Naomi Lind Boccio Designs
110 W. 40th Street/#1007
New York, NY 10018

Ann Sherwin Bromberg
44 Washington Street/#1005
Brookline, MA 02146

Linda Leslie Brown
49 Melcher Street
Boston, MA 02110

Eugenia Butler
P.O. Box 1026
Pac. Palisades, CA 90272

Joyce Marquess Carey
913 Harrison Street
Madison, WI 53711

Jennifer Mackey
Chia Jen Studo
P.O. Box 469
Scotia, CA 95565

Christopher Hyland Inc.
979 Third Avenue
Suite 1714
New York, NY 10022

Cinnabar Traders
1460 Broadway
New York, NY 10036

Clarence House
111 Eighth Avenue
New York, NY 10011

Conrad Imports
575 10th Street
San Francisco, CA 94103

Michael A. Cummings
175 Fifth Avenue–Suite 2193
New York, NY 10010

Margaret Cusack
124 Hoyt Street/Boerum Hill
Brooklyn, NY 11217

Kurt Delbanco
9 E. 82nd Street
New York, NY 10028

Katharine Parham
Design on Fabric
708 S. State, #1
Champaign, IL 61820

Donghia Furniture/Textiles
485 Broadway
New York, NY 10013

The Fabric Workshop
1100 Vine Street
Philadelphia, PA 19123

Mary Edna Fraser
P.O. Box 12250
Charleston, SC 29412

Audrey Goldstein
315 Newtonville Avenue
Newton, MA 02160

Terry Guzman
659 Glenwood Avenue
Teaneck, NJ 07666

Harlem Textile Works
186 E. 122nd Street
New York, NY 10035

J.M. Lynne Company, Inc.
59 Gilpin Avenue
Smithtown, NY 11787

Jane-Albert Studio, Inc.
16 E. 23rd Street
New York, NY 10010

Janis S. Kanter
1923 W. Dickens
Chicago, IL 60614

Libby Kowalski
CTD Studio
41 Union Sq. W./Suite 502
New York, NY 10003

Knoll Textiles
105 Wooster Street
New York, NY 10012

Janet Kuemmerlein
7701 Canterbury
Prairie Village, KS 66208

Jack Lenor Larsen
41 E. 11th Street
New York, NY 10003

Patti Lynn
666 Greenwich Street
New York, NY 10014

Quentel Mathis
136 Hicks/Apt 2B
Brooklyn, NY 11201

Therese May
651 N. 4th Street
San Jose, CA 95112

Sue McFall
210 E. Center Street
Dunkirk, IN 47336

Gudrun Mertes-Frady
105 Eldrige Street
New York, NY 10002

Dottie Moore
1134 Charlotte Avenue
Rock Hill, SC 29732

The NAMES Project
2362 Market Street
San Francisco, CA 94114

Pallina
388 Elizabeth Street
San Francisco, CA 94114

Marilyn Price
6181 Riverview Drive
Indianapolis, IN 46208

Dominique Ragueneau
925 W. 23rd Street
Los Angeles, CA 90007

Christina Read
247 Centre Street
New York, NY 10013

Renata Rubim
Av. Aquara 446 Conj. 402
Porto Alegre RS 90430
Brazil

Don Ruddy
257 W. 19th
New York, NY 10011

Scalamandré
37-24 24th Street
L.I. City, NY 11101

Schumacher
79 Madison Avenue
New York, NY 10016

Frederic Schwartz
Anderson-Schwartz Architects
40 Hudson Street
New York, NY 10013

Nina Sobell
190 Eldridge Street
New York, NY 10002

Joel Sokolov
32 Laight Street
New York, NY 10013

Sofa Soma
245 Eldridge Street/#3F
New York, NY 10002
Attn: Paul Fanfarillo

Peter and Paul Stasek
Tapestries in Arch. & Space
Neckarpromenade 6,6800
Mannheim I, Germany

Unika Vaev USA
305 E. 63rd Street
New York, NY 10021

Christine Van der Hurd
117 E. 24th Street/10th Floor
New York, NY 10010

Jill Wilcox
28 Marine Avenue/6K
Brooklyn, NY 11209

Sylvia Gentile
Windlines
1450 23rd Street
Santa Monica, CA 90404

John Wolf Decorative Fabrics
261 Fifth Avenue
New York, NY 10016

Rebecca Bluestone
The Woven Image
P.O. Box 4421
Santa Fe, NM 87502